Status and Trends of Wetlands in the Conterminous United States 1986 to 1997

Thomas E. Dahl
U.S. Fish and Wildlife Service
Branch of Habitat Assessment
555 Lester Avenue
Onalaska, Wisconsin 54650

Acknowledgments

Many agencies, institutions, and individuals contributed their time, energy, and expertise to the completion of this report, and the author would like to thank the following for their contributions: Gregory Allord, Marta Anderson, Elizabeth Ciganovich, Gary Latzke, David McCulloch, Dick Vraga, and various personnel from the National Mapping Division, *U.S. Geological Survey*; Don Field, *National Oceanic and Atmospheric Administration*; the Cooperative Fish and Wildlife Research Unit, *South Dakota State University*. Staff of several U.S. Fish and Wildlife Service offices provided extraordinary input to aspects of the study including: Elaine Blok, Kevin Bon, John Cooper, David Dall, Jim Dick, Chuck Elliott, Gary Frazier, Ann Haas, Jonathan Hall, Gerry Jackson, William Knapp, Sheila Kratzer, Christine Nolin, Dennis Peters, Cathleen Short, Mark Steingraeber, Benjamin Tuggle, Robert Willis, and Rich Young.

Technical review of the manuscript was provided by the following experts: Kenneth Bierly, *Oregon Watershed Enhancement Board*; Kenneth Burnham, *Colorado State University*; Marvin Hubbell, *Illinois Department of Natural Resources*; J. Henry Sather, *Professor Emeritus, Western Illinois University*; and Douglas Wilcox, *Great Lakes Science Center, U.S. Geological Survey.*

Publication design and layout of the report were done by the Cartography and Publishing Program, U.S. Geological Survey, Madison, Wisconsin.

This report should be cited as follows:

Dahl, T.E. 2000. Status and trends of wetlands in the conterminous United States 1986 to 1997. U.S. Department of the Interior, Fish and Wildlife Service, Washington, D.C. 82 pp.

Cover photograph: Lac Qui Parle State Wildlife Management Area, Minnesota.

Preface

The U.S. Fish and Wildlife Service is committed to working with others to conserve, protect and enhance fish, wildlife, and plants and their habitats for the continuing benefit of the American people. Wetlands are among the most important and ecologically unique habitats in our Nation, and they provide society with many environmental and economic benefits.

The Emergency Wetlands Resources Act requires the Service to update its wetland status and trends information at ten-year intervals. Data in this and previous status and trends reports provide important long-term trend information about specific changes and places and the overall status of wetlands in the United States. Although there are several programs in the Federal Government that collect environmental data, the Service's effort to monitor wetland trends provides the only comprehensive information of that nature available to a broad range of decision makers and the general public. Data in the Service's wetland status and trends reports are used at all levels of government for resource policy establishment and to assess the efficacy of those policies.

This report presents the most comprehensive, technically advanced, and contemporary effort to track wetlands status and trends on a national scale. Its value has been enhanced by the multi-agency involvement in the study's design, in data collection, and in the peer review of the findings. There is unprecedented recognition of wetland issues at all levels of government and in the private sector. Some readers will use this information to gain insights on the effectiveness of wetland protection measures during the past decade; others will look for opportunities to stem wetland losses and restore wetland acreage and functions in a continuing effort to achieve our resource conservation objectives. By assessing our Nation's progress in attaining wetland policy objectives, this report will serve as an important tool for conserving wetlands and their ecological functions and values in the 21st Century.

Jamie Rappaport Clark

DIRECTOR

Conversion Table

U.S. Customary to Metric

inches (in.)	x	25.40	=	millimeters (mm)
inches (in.)	x	2.54	=	centimeters (cm)
feet (ft)	x	0.3048	=	meters (m)
miles (mi)	x	1.609	=	kilometers (km)
nautical miles (nmi)	x	1.852	=	kilometers (km)
square feet (ft²)	x	0.0929	=	square meters (m²)
square miles (mi²)	x	2.590	=	square kilometers (km²)
acres (A)	x	0.4047	=	hectares (ha)
gallons (gal)	x	3.785	=	liters (L)
cubic feet (ft³)	x	0.02831	=	cubic meters (m³)
acre-feet (A-ft)	x	1233.5	=	cubic meters (m³)
ounces (oz)	x	28.3495	=	grams (g)
pounds (lb)	x	0.4536	=	kilograms (kg)
short tons (tons)	x	0.9072	=	metric tons (t)
British Thermal Units (BTU)	x	0.2520	=	kilocalories (kcal)
Farenheit degrees (F)		0.5556 (F - 32)	=	Celsius degrees (C)

Metric to U.S. Customary

millimeters (mm)	x	0.03937	=	inches (in.)
centimeters (cm)	x	0.3937	=	inches (in.)
meters (m)	x	3.281	=	feet (ft)
kilometers (km)	x	0.6214	=	miles (mi)
square meters (m²)	x	10.764	=	square feet (ft²)
square kilometers (km²)	x	0.3861	=	square miles (mi²)
hectares (ha)	x	2.471	=	acres (A)
liters (L)	x	0.2642	=	gallons (gal)
cubic meters (m³)	x	35.31	=	cubic feet (ft³)
cubic meters (m³)	x	0.0008110	=	acre-feet (A-ft)
milligrams (mg)	x	0.00003527	=	ounces (oz)
grams (g)	x	0.03527	=	ounces (oz)
kilograms (kg)	x	2.2046	=	ounces (oz)
metric tons (t)	x	2204.62	=	pounds (lb)
metric tons (t)	x	1.102	=	short tons (tons)
kilocalories (kcal)	x	3.968	=	British Thermal Units (BTU)
Celsius degrees (C)		1.8(C) + 32	=	Farenheit degrees (F)

Contents

List of Figures

List of Tables

Executive Summary

At the time of European settlement, the area that is now the conterminous United States contained an estimated 221 million acres (89.5 million ha) of wetlands. Over time, wetlands have been drained, dredged, filled, leveled, and flooded to the extent that less than half of the original wetland acreage remains (Dahl 1990).

The U.S. Fish and Wildlife Service's first wetlands status and trends report (Frayer *et al.* 1983) estimated the rate of wetland conversion between the mid 1950s and the mid 1970s at 458,000 acres (185,400 ha) per year. Those estimates captured trends from the period preceding many efforts to protect and restore wetlands. Society's views about wetlands have changed considerably and interest in the preservation of wetlands has increased as the values of wetlands have become more fully understood.

Evidence of progress in reducing wetland losses became apparent in the Service's updated status and trends report (Dahl and Johnson 1991) covering the mid 1970s to the mid 1980s. The estimated rate of wetland loss had declined to 290,000 acres (117,400 ha) per year.

In 1986, the Emergency Wetlands Resources Act of 1986 (Public Law 99-645) was enacted to promote the conservation of our Nation's wetlands. The Act requires the Service to conduct wetland status and trend studies of the Nation's wetlands at 10-year intervals. This report to the Congress details the status and trends of our Nation's wetlands from 1986 to 1997. It provides the most recent and comprehensive estimates of the current status and trends of wetland habitats.

An interagency group of statisticians developed the design for the national status and trends study. The study design consists of 4,375 randomly selected sample plots. Each plot is four square miles (2,560 acres or 1,040 ha) in area. These plots were examined, with the use of recent remotely sensed data in combination with field work, to determine wetland change. Twenty-one percent of the plots were field verified, and rigorous quality control measures were taken to ensure data integrity and quality. Estimates were made of wetland area by wetland type and changes over time.

The study incorporated all wetlands, regardless of land ownership, as part of the sampled landscape. Because wetlands in coastal areas are important to a variety of fish and wildlife species, this study included them by adding a supplemental sampling stratum along the Atlantic and Gulf coastal fringes.

Determining what caused wetland loss or gains is an important part of assessing the effectiveness of policy or management actions. As part of this study, the Service worked with other Federal agencies to examine and field test wetland loss and gain attribution categories. Wetland losses and gains have been assigned to five general categories: upland urban development, upland agriculture, upland silviculture, upland rural development, and other miscellaneous lands.

National Status

An estimated 105.5 million acres (42.7 million ha) of wetlands remained in the conterminous United States in 1997. Between 1986 and 1997, the net loss of wetlands was 644,000 acres (260,700 ha). The annual loss rate during this period was 58,500 acres (23,700 ha), which represents an eighty percent reduction in the average annual rate of wetland loss as compared to the last wetlands status and trends report. Various factors have contributed to the decline in the loss rate including implementation and enforcement of wetland protection measures and elimination of some incentives for wetland drainage. Public education and outreach about the value and functions of wetlands, private land initiatives, coastal monitoring and protection programs, and wetland restoration and creation actions have also helped reduce overall wetland losses.

Ninety-five percent of the remaining wetlands were inland freshwater wetlands. Five percent of the Nation's wetlands were in saltwater estuarine environments. Freshwater forested wetlands made up the single largest category (50.7 million acres or 20.5 million ha) of all wetlands in the conterminous United States.

Estuarine and Marine Wetlands

Three categories of estuarine and marine wetlands were included in this study: estuarine intertidal emergents such as salt and brackish water marshes; estuarine shrubs such as mangroves and other salt tolerant woody species; and estuarine and marine intertidal non-vegetated wetlands such as beaches, tidal flats, shoals, sand spits, and bars. These wetlands provide valuable nursery, feeding, breeding, staging, and resting areas for an array of fishes, shellfish, mammals, and birds. These resources face a dual threat from natural stressors such as storms, wind and wave erosion, land subsidence, and sea level rise, and from pressure brought about by human population increases in coastal counties.

An estimated 5.3 million acres (2.2 million ha) of marine and estuarine intertidal wetlands made up about 5 percent of the total wetland acreage in the conterminous United States. Vegetated estuarine wetlands made up an estimated 87 percent of estuarine wetlands. Non-vegetated estuarine and marine wetlands (see Appendix A) including beaches, flats, and shoals, made up 13 percent of all intertidal wetlands or 711,000 acres (287,900 ha).

Estuarine and marine wetlands accounted for two percent of the total loss of all wetlands observed in this study. Between 1986 and 1997 there was a net loss of 10,400 acres (4,200 ha) of estuarine and marine

wetlands; an estimated annual loss of about 1,000 acres (405 ha). The rate of loss for these wetlands was reduced more than 82 percent from the previous decade. This was the result of various Federal and State agencies that have contributed to restoration, protection and monitoring of coastal areas.

Long-term trends indicate that estuarine vegetated wetland area declined at a much reduced rate from earlier decades, and that non-vegetated wetland types have remained fairly constant over time.

Freshwater Wetlands

Freshwater wetlands support a variety of fish and wildlife species and contribute to the aesthetic and environmental quality in every State. Millions of Americans use freshwater wetlands annually for hunting, fishing, bird watching and other outdoor activities.

An estimated 100.2 million acres (40.6 million ha) of freshwater wetlands of various types remain in the conterminous United States. There were 50.7 million acres (20.5 million ha) of forested wetlands, 25.2 million acres (10.2 million ha) of freshwater emergents, and 18.4 million acres (7.5 million ha) of freshwater shrub wetlands. There were also an estimated 5.5 million acres (2.2 million ha) of freshwater ponds.

Ninety-eight percent of all losses recorded during this study were to freshwater wetlands. The net loss of all freshwater wetland types was 633,500 acres (256,500 ha). Freshwater forested wetlands and freshwater emergent marshes each lost an estimated 1.2 million acres (486,000 ha) between 1986 and 1997. The numeric losses of freshwater wetlands were partially offset by gains in freshwater shrub wetlands (1.1 million acres or 445,000 ha) and freshwater ponds (631,000 acres or 256,000 ha).

The freshwater shrub category was the only vegetated freshwater wetland type to increase in area between 1986 and 1997.

The open water pond category gained the most area since the 1950s. There were 5.5 million acres (2.2 million ha) of open water ponds in 1997. This was more than twice the area of open water ponds reported in the mid 1950s. Nationally, the lower Mississippi Valley and central Florida contributed substantially to the number of larger ponds created by human activities. Many of the larger ponds in the Mississippi Valley were created for aquaculture. Ponds in central Florida were either water retention ponds associated with development or sediment retention basins related to surface mining operations.

The long-term trends in freshwater wetlands since the 1950s, show that freshwater emergent wetlands have declined by the greatest percentage of all wetland types with nearly 24 percent lost (8 million acres or 3.2 million ha). Freshwater forested wetlands have sustained the greatest overall loss in area, declining by 10.4 million acres (4.2 million ha).

Freshwater Lakes and Reservoirs
Freshwater lakes and reservoirs are deepwater habitats that provide recreation for millions of people. They support inland fisheries and are stopover locations for many migratory birds.

Between 1986 and 1997, deepwater lakes and reservoirs exhibited a modest increase in area with a net gain of 116,400 acres (47,100 ha). The rate of lake and reservoir creation declined 43 percent from the 1970s to 1980s.

Attribution of Wetland Losses and Gains

This report indicates that urban development accounted for 30 percent of the loss of wetland to upland land use categories from 1986 to 1997; 26 percent of the loss was attributed to agriculture; 23 percent to silviculture and 21 percent to rural development.

Estuarine and Marine Wetlands
The major factor in estuarine and marine wetland loss was filling or draining for development. Together, urban and rural development accounted for 43 percent of the estuarine and marine wetland losses.

Seventy five percent of all estuarine and marine losses occurred in emergent salt marsh wetlands. Emergent salt marshes declined by an estimated 14,450 acres (5,850 ha), a 0.4 percent loss. Fifty-eight percent of these losses were from some form of deepwater intrusion into the salt marsh. Estuarine shrub wetlands increased slightly with a net gain of about 6,600 acres (2,670 ha). Most of this increase was the result of conversions from other estuarine wetland types. The loss in estuarine non-vegetated wetlands (flats, bars and shoals) was not statistically significant (less than 1 percent of all estuarine wetland losses).

Yosemite National Park, California.

Freshwater Wetlands

Urban development accounted for 30 percent of the estimated losses in the freshwater system. Twenty-six percent of the loss was attributable to agriculture; 23 percent to silviculture, and 21 percent to rural development. The rate of freshwater wetland loss on agricultural lands declined substantially from the previous decade. Previously, about 1.0 million acres (404,900 ha) were lost to agriculture as opposed to 198,000 acres (80,200 ha) during 1986 to 1997. However, freshwater emergent wetlands in agricultural areas, especially those that are partially drained, continue to be lost. Implementation of the wetland conservation provisions in the Food Security Act, as amended, and agricultural set-aside and land retirement programs may have contributed to the reduction in wetland loss rate.

Collectively, 51 percent or 383,300 acres (155,200 ha) of all the freshwater wetlands lost to uplands resulted from urban expansion or rural development such as the construction of buildings, roads, bridges and other infrastructure in wetlands. Freshwater non-tidal wetlands experienced substantial development pressure just inland from the coastlines of the United States.

Freshwater emergent wetlands experienced substantial losses of more than 1.2 million acres (496,400 ha). This was a reduction of 4.7 percent. Of the 700,000 acres (283,000 ha) of emergent wetlands lost to upland, an estimated 51 percent were on agricultural lands. Another 22 percent were lost to development in urban or rural settings, 25 percent to unidentified land uses, and 2 percent were converted to silviculture.

Substantial inroads were made during this study period in curtailing overall wetland losses and in restoring or creating wetland area. Progress was also made in reducing the loss of estuarine wetlands along our coastlines. The number of forested wetlands converted to agriculture was reduced in areas like the lower Mississippi alluvial plain and the coastal plain of the southeastern United States. Federal programs such as the conservation provisions of the Food Security Act, the Fish & Wildlife Service's coastal programs and conservation partnership programs have contributed to the declining wetland loss rate.

A freshwater wetland in northern Wisconsin.

Introduction

The mission of the U. S. Fish and Wildlife Service is to conserve, protect, and enhance fish, wildlife and plants and their habitats for the continuing benefit of the American people. The Service has trust responsibilities for migratory birds, endangered species, anadromous and interjurisdictional fisheries, and some marine mammals. The Service also manages the National Wildlife Refuge System that protects and conserves a myriad of the Nation's wetland habitats.

Wetlands are crucial for many species and they provide benefits to people. In recent years, public appreciation of the ecological, social and economic values of wetlands has increased substantially (The Conservation Foundation 1988). The increased awareness of how much wetland acreage has been lost or damaged since the time of European settlement, and the consequences of those losses has led to the development of many Federal, State, and local wetland protection programs and laws. Several landmark pieces of legislation, Presidential Executive orders, and agency programs have contributed positively to wetland conservation efforts. There have also been regional wetland loss studies conducted that help identify important wetland trends and contribute to regional management priorities.

The Emergency Wetlands Resources Act (Public Law 99-645) was enacted to promote the conservation of our Nation's wetlands. Congress recognized that wetlands are nationally significant resources and that these resources have been affected by human activities. The Act requires the Service to conduct wetland status and trend studies of the Nation's wetlands at 10-year intervals. Earlier reports on wetland status and trends include Frayer *et al.* (1983), Tiner (1984), Dahl (1990), and Dahl and Johnson (1991).

This report to the Congress details the status and trends of our Nation's wetlands. It covers the period from 1986 to 1997, and provides the most recent and comprehensive estimates of the current status of wetland area throughout the conterminous United States and the losses or gains to various wetland types that have occurred during this time.

New technology contributed to the information presented in this report. Geospatial analysis capability now built into the status and trends study provided a complete digital database to assist in analyzing wetland change information. This information has important resource policy implications to help managers interpret the role that wetlands play on the national landscape. It also provided the Service and its partners with scientific data to help guide resource management decisions on wetland related issues such as restoration and enhancement, endangered species habitat availability and ecosystem management planning. The data currently available provide a half-century record of wetland change beginning with the first status and trends report that covered the 1950s to 1970s.

This study provides a quantitative measure of the areal extent of all wetlands in the conterminous United States. The study provides no qualitative assessments of wetland functions.

Study Design and Procedures

Study Area

The total land area of the conterminous United States is about 1.93 billion acres (0.8 billion ha). The topography ranges from mountainous terrain to low relief coastal plains and river deltas. Climate and geography influence habitats that vary from deserts to subtropical conditions. Although wetlands occur in every State and physiographic region, there are obvious differences in their abundance between regions. Stratification of the Nation based on the differences in wetland density makes this study an effective measure of wetland resources.

Some Federal inventories stop at county boundaries or at a point coinciding with the census line for inhabitable land area. Doing so may exclude offshore wetlands, shallow water embayments or sounds, shoals, sand bars, tidal flats and reefs (Figure 1). These are important fish and wildlife habitats. Consequently, the Service included wetlands in coastal areas by adding a supplemental sampling stratum along the Atlantic and Gulf coastal fringes. This zone includes the near shore areas of the coast with its barrier islands, coastal marshes, exposed tidal flats and other offshore features not a part of the landward physiographic zones. The coastal zone stratum, as described

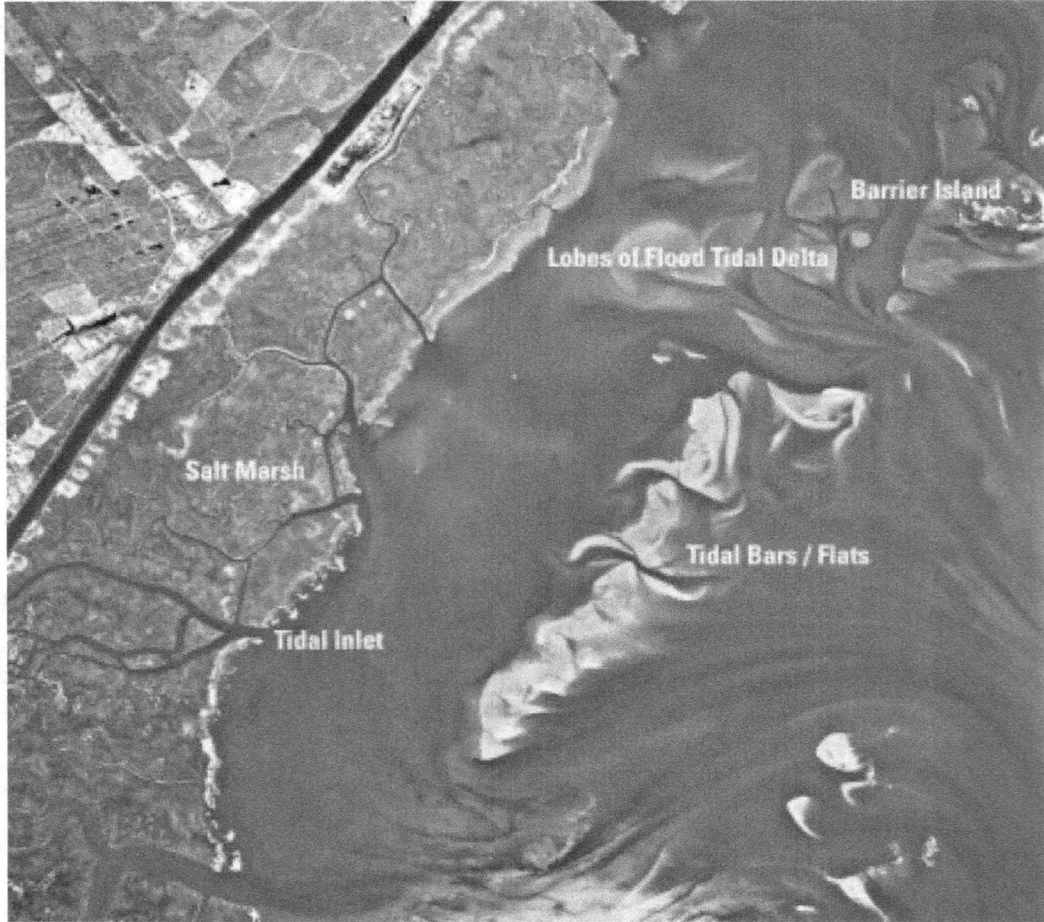

Figure 1. A 1999 color infrared aerial photograph of the coastal region of Bull Island, South Carolina. Wetland features such as sand flats, inter-tidal bars, shoals, and small islands were important wetland habitats included within a coastal zone stratum. (National Aerial Photography Program.)

14

here, included almost 28.2 million acres (11.4 million ha). At its widest point in southern Louisiana, this zone extended about 92.6 miles (149 km) from Lake Pontchartrain to the furthest extent of estuarine wetland resources. It was an area where saltwater is the overriding influence on biological systems. The coastal zone in this study was not synonymous with any State or Federal jurisdictional coastal zone definitions. The legal definition of "coastal zone" has been developed for use in coastal demarcations, planning, regulatory and management activities undertaken by other Federal or State agencies.

Wetland Definition and Classification

The Service uses the Cowardin et al. (1979) definition of wetland. This definition is the standard for the agency and is the national standard for wetland mapping, monitoring and data reporting as determined by the Federal Geographic Data Committee. This definition has been used for the present study as well as previous wetland status and trends reports. It is a two-part definition as indicated below:

"Wetlands are lands transitional between terrestrial and aquatic systems where the water table is usually at or near the surface or the land is covered by shallow water.

For purposes of this classification wetlands must have one or more of the following three attributes: (1) at least periodically, the land supports predominantly hydrophytes, (2) the substrate is predominantly undrained hydric soil, and (3) the substrate is nonsoil and is saturated with water or covered

Table 1: Wetland, deepwater and upland categories used in this study. The definitions for each category appear in Appendix A.

Category	Common Description
Salt Water Habitats	
Marine Subtidal*	Open ocean
Marine Intertidal	Near shore
Estuarine Subtidal*	Open water/bay bottoms
Estuarine Intertidal Emergents	Salt marsh
Estuarine Intertidal Forested/Shrub	Mangroves or other estuarine shrubs
Estuarine Intertidal Unconsolidated Shore	Beaches/bars
Estuarine Aquatic Bed**	Submerged or floating estuarine vegetation
Riverine (may be tidal or non-tidal)*	River systems
Freshwater Habitats	
Palustrine Forested	Forested swamps
Palustrine Shrub	Shrub wetlands
Palustrine Emergents	Inland marshes/wet meadows
Palustrine Unconsolidated Shore	Shore beaches/bars
Palustrine Unconsolidated Bottom	Open water ponds
Palustrine Aquatic Bed	Floating aquatic/submerged vegetation
Lacustrine*	Lakes and reservoirs
Uplands	
Agriculture	Cropland, pasture, managed rangeland
Urban	Cities and incorporated developments
Forested Plantations	Planted or intensively managed forests; silviculture
Rural Development	Non-urban developed areas and infrastructure
Other Uplands	Rural uplands not in any other category; barren lands

* Constitutes deepwater habitat
** Technical limitations described in the text

by shallow water at some time during the growing season of each year."

Habitat category definitions are given in synoptic form in Table 1. The reader is encouraged to review Appendices A and B, which provide complete definitions of wetland types and land use categories used in this study as well as a comparison of wetland definitions and habitat types that may be treated differently by other Federal agencies.

Study Design

An interagency group of statisticians developed the design for the national status and trends study. The basic sampling design and study objectives have remained constant for each wetland status and trends report. The study design consists of 4,375 randomly selected sample plots. Each plot is four square miles (2,560 acres or 1,040 ha) in area. The plots were examined, with the use of remotely sensed data in combination with field work, to determine wetland change. Estimates of change in wetlands were made over a specific time period.

To determine changes in wetland area, the 48 conterminous States were stratified or divided by State boundaries and 35 physiographic subdivisions described by Hammond (1970) and shown in Figure 2. To permit even spatial coverage of the sample, the 36 physiographic regions formed by the Hammond

1	Coast Ranges
2	Puget Willamette Lowland
3	Cascade Klamath Sierra Nevada Ranges
4	Central Valley of California
5	Columbia Basin
6	Blue Mountains
7	Harney and Owyhee Broken Lands
8	Basin and Range Area
9	Northern Rocky Mountains
10	Snake River Lowland
11	Middle Rocky Mountains
12	Wyoming Big Horn Basins
13	Colorado River Plateaus
14	Upper Gila Mountains
15	North Central Lake Swamp Moraine Plains
16	Upper Missouri Basin Broken Lands

17	Southern Rocky Mountains
18	Rocky Mountain Piedmont
19	High Plains
20	Stockton Balcones Escarpment
21	Dakota Minnesota Drift and Lake Bed Flats
22	Nebraska Sand Hills
23	West Central Rolling Hills
24	Midcontinent Plains and Escarpments
25	Southwest Wisconsin Hills
26	Middle Western Upland Plain

27	Ozark Ouachita Highlands
28	Lower Mississippi Alluvial Plain
29	East Central Drift and Lake Bed Flats
30	Eastern Interior Uplands and Basins
31	Appalachian Highlands
32	Adirondack New England Highlands
33	Lower New England
34	Gulf Atlantic Rolling Plain
35	Gulf Atlantic Coastal Flats
36	Coastal Zone

Figure 2. The physiographic regions of the conterminous United States. A coastal zone stratum (zone 36) has been added to this study (Source: Hammond 1970).

subdivisions and the coastal zone stratum were intersected with State boundaries to form 220 subdivisions or strata. An example of this stratification approach and the way it related to sampling frequency is shown in Figure 3.

In the physiographic strata described above, weighted, stratified sample plots were randomly allocated in proportion to the amount of wetland acreage expected to occur in each stratum. Each sample area was a surface plot 2.0 miles (3.2 km) on a side or 4 square miles of area equaling 2,560 acres (1,036 ha). Plots were initially allocated to strata based on the best information available about wetland area and variability by strata and on a standard optimal-allocation formula for stratified simple-random sampling when the study was initiated in 1978. Because declining wetland loss rates require more finite measurement techniques to ensure a high degree of statistical reliability, the sample size of this study was augmented with additional sample plots.

For the present study, about 725 supplemental sample plots were added to parts of Maine, Vermont, New York, Pennsylvania, Ohio, West Virginia, Kentucky, Tennessee, Nebraska, Kansas, Oklahoma, New Mexico, Arizona, Nevada, Washington, and three physiographic zones of the northern Rocky Mountains and the Snake River Lowlands in Wyoming, Montana, and Idaho. As sample plot locations were geographically referenced for positional accuracy, some plots were moved to other strata based on their true earth coordinates. In these instances, additional plots were added at random in the affected strata to ensure a consistent sample size. Wetland changes were determined by intensive analysis of the imagery,

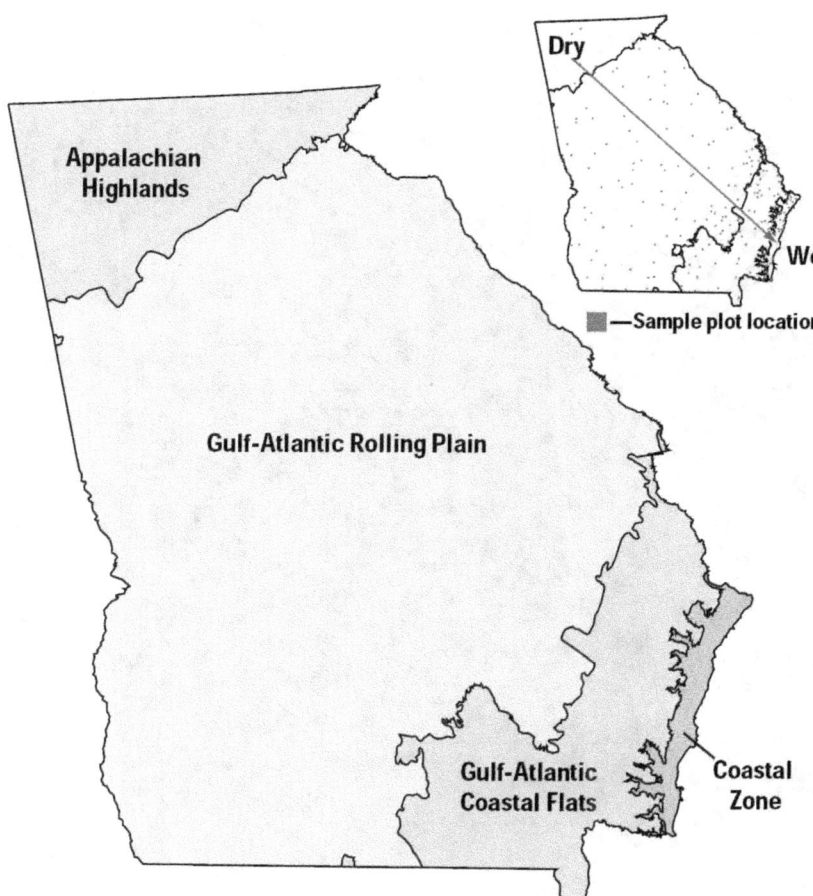

Figure 3. Statification based on physiographic regions and a coastal zone stratum in Georgia. The sample plot density increased in relation to wetland area, from drier (Appalachian Highlands) to wetter (Coastal Zone). This stratification scheme has ecological and statistical advantages.

interpretation of wetland types and hydrologic conditions, and determination of the changes that occurred between the respective target dates. The study was designed to produce estimates of total wetland area and changes for the conterminous United States.

The procedures follow U.S. Fish and Wildlife Service (1994a, 1994b). An advantage to this design was that it focused entirely on monitoring wetland change, and it was used to monitor conversions between ecologically different wetland types, and measure wetland gains and losses.

Imagery

Previous studies have used aerial imagery to monitor wetland changes over time (Hefner *et al.* 1994; Moulton *et al.* 1997; Dahl 1999; and others). This study used multiple sources of recent imagery and direct on-the-ground observations to record wetland change information.

An agency decision required the use of imagery with a mean date no older than 1997. Traditionally, the Service relied on aerial photography available from the National Aerial Photography Program (NAPP) for making wetland change detection assessments. Although the NAPP imagery still forms a large part of the source information, NAPP coverage dated 1997 or more recent, was not available for all sample plot areas. To achieve complete coverage and meet the target date required, this study used imagery provided by five Federal agencies, four State agencies, and one private organization.

The mean imagery date for each of the States is shown in Figure 4. West Virginia and Florida were the two exceptions that retained mean imagery dates earlier than 1997. It was not practicable to update sample plots to reflect current conditions by using direct field examination in these two States because most of the West Virginia sample plots were inaccessible and many plots in Florida contained changes too

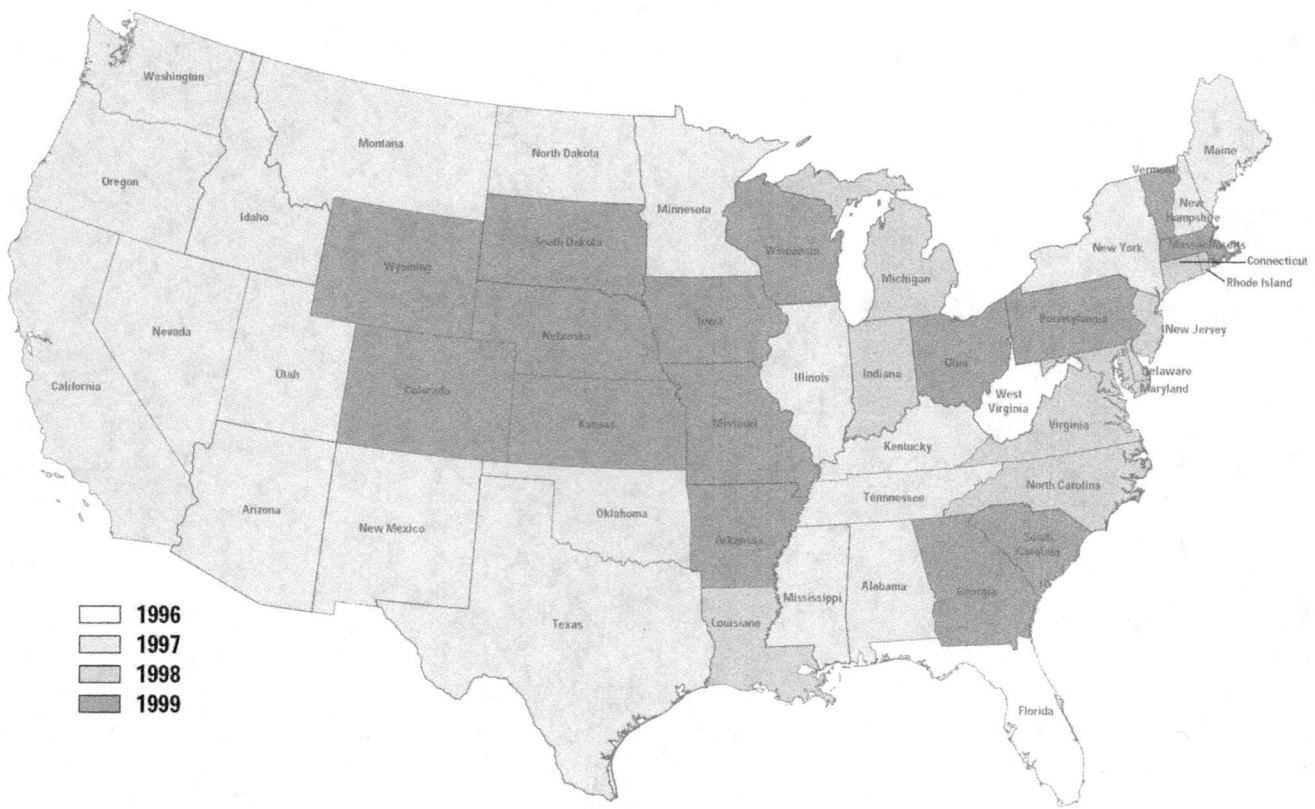

Figure 4. Mean dates of imagery used to update wetlands in each of the conterminous United States.

numerous and extensive to accurately portray on anything other than a recent image base.

Imagery, in the form of aerial photographs, ranged in scale and type; most was 1:40,000 scale, color infrared. Only the most recent, good quality imagery was used. In some instances, customized flights were made to acquire good quality photography.

Early spring and late fall (leaf-off) imagery was usually used. The determination of the extent of forested wetlands can be difficult and there were distinct advantages to using leaf-off imagery to detect the extent of forested wetlands. Visual evidence of hydrologic conditions such as saturation, flooding or ponding combined with collateral data sources such as soil surveys, topographic maps and wetland maps were used to identify and delineate the areal extent of forested wetlands. Early spring and late fall imagery was an important tool in this process.

The study included all wetlands regardless of land ownership. All wetlands 3 acres (1.2 ha) and larger composed the target population. The results indicate that for each wetland category included, the minimum size represented was less than 1.0 acres (0.4 ha). However, not all wetlands less than the target size category were detected. For each sample plot, the rate of change among all wetland types between the two dates of imagery was used to estimate the total area of the sample plot in each wetland type and the changes in wetland area between these dates. The changes were recorded in categories that can be considered the result of either natural change, such as the natural succession of emergent wetlands to shrub wetlands, or human-induced change. Areas of the sample plot that had been identified in previous eras as wetlands but that were no longer wetlands, were placed into five land use categories including agriculture, upland forested plantations, upland areas of rural development, upland urban landscapes, and other miscellaneous lands. The outputs from this analysis were change matrices that provided estimates of wetland area by type and observed changes over time. As in past studies, rigorous quality control inspections were built into the interpretation, data collection and analysis processes.

Field Verification

Field verification was completed for 912 (21 percent) of the sample plots distributed in 35 States (Figure 5). This constituted the largest field verification effort undertaken for a status and trends report.

Field verification addressed questions regarding image interpretation, land use coding and attribution of wetland gains or losses. Field work was also done as a quality control measure to verify that plot delineations were correct. Verification involved field visits to a cross section of wetland types and geographical settings, and to plots with different image types, scales and dates. Field work was used to update sample plots based on observations of on-the-ground conditions. Representatives from six Federal agencies participated in field reconnaissance trips from April 1999 through May 2000.

Technological Advances

Advances in computerized cartography were used to improve data quality and geospatial integrity. In past studies, annotated images were manually transferred to a topographic base map scale using a zoom transfer scope. Area measurement and change information were obtained from a transfer overlay at 1:24,000 scale by either scanning or board digitization. That process required human intervention to retrace lines three times: once during the photographic interpretation process, once during the rectification to base map scale process, and finally for area measurement or board digitizing.

Newer technologies allowed the generation of existing digital plot files at any scale to overlay directly onto an image base. The wetlands interpreter viewed the new imagery stereoscopically and made change notations directly on the image overlay. The change overlay was then rescanned. Because the plot information was already in a spatially rectified file, any change information could be inserted to the correct geospatial position in the plot boundary. Area information was recalculated from the new digital file by use of a geographic information system. This process eliminated manual drafting, registered the image overlays to georeferenced coordinates, and reduced imprecise lines (line pixel width) inherent in older scanning technologies.

The geospatial analysis capability built into this study provided a complete digital database to better assist analysis of wetland change information.

Quality Control and Quality Assurance

A quality assurance program is essential for ensuring the validity of analytical data (U.S. EPA 1979). The Service has developed and implemented quality assurance measures that provide appropriate methods to take field measurements, ensure sample integrity and provide oversight of analyses which included reporting of procedural and statistical confidence levels.

The objective of this study was to produce comprehensive, statistically valid acreage estimates of the Nation's wetlands. Because of the sample based approach, various quality control and quality assurance measures were built into the data collection, review, analysis and reporting stages. Some of the major quality control steps were:

Plot Location and Positional Accuracy

Status and trends sample plots were permanently fixed georeferenced areas that are revisited periodically to monitor land use and cover type changes. The plot coordinates were positioned precisely using a system of redundant backup locators on prints produced from a geographic information system, topographic maps, other maps used for collateral information and the aerial imagery. Plot outlines were computer generated for the correct spatial coordinates, size and projection. Plot locations were transferred and registered onto all work materials.

Figure 5. Sample plots were field verified in parts of 35 States from April 1999 to May 2000.

Imagery, Base Maps and Collateral Data

Aerial imagery was the primary data source, but it was used with reliable collateral data such as topographic maps, coastal navigation charts, published soil surveys, published wetland maps, and State, local or regional studies. All photography was cataloged, numbered, tagged, and tracked in a database management system.

Photo Interpretation Quality Control Review

Determination of wetland change characteristics from aerial imagery requires a high level of accuracy in the identification and classification of wetlands, deepwater habitats and associated uplands. Because of the complexity and the amount of data to be viewed and processed, accurate wetland interpretation from aerial imagery requires considerable expertise. A small cadre of highly trained and experienced wetlands interpreters completed the image analysis. Wetland image interpreters averaged 12 years of wetlands interpretation and classification experience. This ensured high quality, accurate and nationally consistent data.

Image interpreters conducted field verification exercises to ensure accurate and consistent interpretation of imagery and to resolve various interpretation questions. Quality control field trip reports and field data sheets provided documentation of field reconnaissance efforts, general descriptions of wetlands and uplands in an area, descriptions of surface water conditions both on the imagery and at the time of field work, and details about the quality of the source materials used.

Quality control reviews were conducted by an experienced photo interpreter other than the individual responsible for the original work. Stereoscopic quality control reviews of all photo interpretation work were conducted for each sample plot. These reviews involved checking for errors of omitted wetlands, identification of false changes (such as drought or draw-down conditions), classification errors, unlabeled polygon features, incomplete work and agreement with collateral data sources. Documented procedural specifications and conventions assisted in quality control reviews. This documentation and a complete description of the techniques used to accomplish the photo interpretation and change detection process are provided in various technical manuals (U.S. Fish and Wildlife Service 1994a; 1994b).

Change Information and Data Capture

Color differential scanning (see "Technological Advances") of plot change data eliminated much of the manual cartographic transfer and

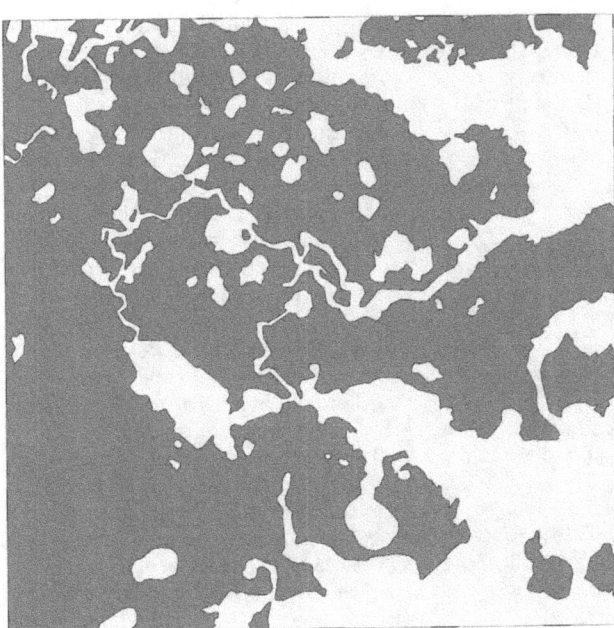

Figure 6. A color-coded digital review plot from coastal New Jersey. These interim work products were used as part of the quality control process.

digitizing work of past studies. The scanning technique was used to capture changes of plot features, cartographically register the revised plot information, and determine area measurement, all in an automated format. This minimized inaccuracies in the process, and it facilitated the use of interim review plots as an additional quality control step. The utility of an interim color-coded digital review plot to assist with the inspection of polygonal data, classification coding, and spatial integrity of the data in the plot boundaries is shown in Figure 6. Unlabeled polygons were eliminated and area measurements became more precise by automating the data capture process.

Quality Assurance of Digital Data Files

All digital data files were subjected to rigorous quality control inspections. Automated checking modules incorporated in the geographic information system (ARC/INFO) were used to correct digital artifacts including vector dangles, undershoots, overshoots, unclosed polygons, and incorrectly coded polygons. Additional customized data inspections were made to ensure that the changes indicated at the image interpretation stage were properly executed. Digital file quality control reviews also provided confirmation of plot location, stratum assignment, and total land or water area sampled.

Database Logic Checks

Logic checking used a series of customized database queries designed to eliminate potential errors in plot geophysical address information, attribute coding, improbable change data or impossible feature classification.

Statistical Sampling and Analysis

The wetland status and trends study was based on a scientific probability sample of the surface area of the 48 conterminous States. The area sampled was about 1.93 billion acres (0.8 billion ha), and the sampling did not discriminate based on land ownership. The study used a stratified, simple random sampling design.

About 754,000 possible sample plots comprised the total population. Given this population, the sampling design was stratified by use of the 36 physical subdivisions described in the "Study Design" section. This stratification scheme had ecological, statistical, and practical advantages. This study design was well suited for determining wetland acreage trends because the 36 divisions of the United States coincide with factors that effect wetland distribution and abundance. Once stratified, the land subdivisions represented very large areas, and it was desirable, on statistical-scientific principles, to achieve a more even spatial spread to the sample plots. The final stratification, which was based on intersecting physiographic land types with state boundaries, guaranteed an improved spatial random sample of plots.

Geographic information system software was used to organize the information about the 4,375 random sample plots. An important design feature crucial to understanding the technical aspects of this study is that a grid of full-sized square plots can be overlaid on any stratum to define the population of sampling units for that stratum. However, at the stratum boundaries some plots were "split" across the boundary and thus, were not a full 2,560 acres (1,036 ha). In sampling theory, plot size is an auxiliary variable that is known for all sampled plots and whose total is known over every stratum. All sampling units (plots) in a stratum were given equal selection probabilities regardless of their size. In the data analysis phase, the adjustments were made for varying plot sizes by use of ratio estimation theory. For any wetland type, the proportion of its area in the sample of plots in a stratum was an unbiased estimator of the unknown proportion of that type in that stratum.

Inference about total wetland acreage by wetland type or for all wetlands in any stratum began with the ratio (r) of the relevant total acreage observed in the sample (Ty), for that stratum divided by the total area of the sample (Tx). Thus, y was measured in each sample plot; $r = Ty/Tx$, and the estimated total acreage of the relevant wetland type in the stratum was A x r. The sum of these estimated totals over all strata provided the national estimate for the wetland type in question.

Uncertainty, which was measured as sampling variance of an estimate, was estimated based on the variation among the sample proportions in a stratum (the estimation of sample variation is highly technical and not presented here). The sampling variation of the national total was the sum of the sampling variance over all strata. These methods are standard for ratio estimation in association with a stratified random sampling design (Sarndal et al. 1992; Thompson 1992).

By use of this statistical procedure, the sample plot data were expanded to specific physiographic regions, by wetland type, and statistical estimates were generated for the 48 conterminous States. The reliability of each estimate generated is expressed as the percent coefficient of variation (% C.V.) associated with that estimate. Percent coefficient of variation was expressed as (standard deviation/mean)x(100). The percent coefficient of variation indicates that there was a 95 percent probability that an estimate was within the indicated percentage range of the true value.

Procedural Error and Statistical Error

Procedural or measurement errors are foreign to the notion of statistical probability, but they occur in the data collection phase of any study and must be considered. Although statistical reliability refers to the ability to replicate results, the concept is conditional on the accuracy of the measurements. A well designed statistical study may still produce erroneous results if the procedural error is unacceptable.

Procedural error was related to the ability to accurately recognize and classify wetlands both from multiple sources of imagery and on-the-ground evaluations. Types of procedural errors were missed wetlands, inclusion of upland as wetland, misclassification of wetlands, or misinterpretation of data collection protocols. The amount of introduced procedural

error is usually a function of the quality of the data-collection conventions; the number, variability, training and experience of data collection personnel; and the rigor of any quality control or quality assurance measures. This study used well established, time-tested, fully documented data collection conventions (U.S. Fish and Wildlife Service 1994a; 1994b). It employed a small cadre of highly skilled and experienced personnel for data collection and processing. Rigorous quality control reviews and redundant inspections were incorporated into the data collection and data entry processes to help reduce the level of procedural error. Estimated procedural error ranged from 4 to 6 percent of the true values when all quality assurance measures had been completed.

Study Limitations

Certain habitats were excluded from this study because of the limitations of aerial imagery as the primary data source to detect wetlands. This was consistent with previous wetland status and trends studies conducted by the Service. These habitats included seagrasses or submerged aquatic vegetation that are found in the intertidal and subtidal zones of estuaries and near shore coastal waters (Orth et al. 1990). The detection of submerged aquatic vegetation using aerial imagery is difficult without extensive surface-level observations, tide-stage data, water-clarity data and because of surface waves (Ferguson et al. 1993). Because of these requirements, the majority of seagrasses were not delineated as part of this study, and the data presented in this report are not intended to provide a reliable indicator of the extent of seagrass area in coastal waters of the conterminous United States. A supplemental discussion of seagrasses as estuarine and marine wetland types is provided.

Unlike the broad expanses of emergent wetlands along the Gulf and Atlantic coasts, the estuarine wetlands of California, Oregon and Washington occur in discontinuous pockets. Their patchy distribution precludes establishment of a coastal stratum as exists for Gulf and Atlantic coast wetlands and no statistically valid data could be obtained through establishment of a coastal stratum there. Therefore, consistent with past studies, this study did not sample Pacific coast estuarine wetlands such as those in San Francisco Bay, California; Coos Bay, Oregon, or Puget Sound, Washington.

Ephemeral wetlands are not recognized as a wetland type by Cowardin et al. (1979), and were not included in this study. These areas have not been included in any of the Service's previous reports.

Wetlands that were farmed periodically during dry years, but under normal circumstances support hydrophytic vegetation (e.g., seasonally flooded wetlands that were periodically farmed for wheat production on the Northern Great Plains) are classified as freshwater emergent wetland in this study.

Effectively drained palustrine wetlands observed in farm production were not considered wetland in the Service's estimated base wetland acreage. For example, throughout the southeastern United States and in California, rice (Oryza sativa) is planted on drained hydric soils and on upland soils. When rice is actively being grown, the land was flooded with water and the area functions as a wetland. In years when rice was not grown, the same fields were used to grow other crops (e.g., corn, soybeans, cotton). An estimated 12 million acres (4.9 million ha) of commercial rice lands were identified primarily in California, Arkansas, Louisiana, Mississippi and Texas. These cultivated rice fields were not able to support hydrophytic vegetation and be included as palustrine farmed wetland under the Cowardin et al. (1979) definition. Therefore, the Service did not include these lands in the base wetland acreage estimates.

Emergent and floating vegetation.

Freshwater wetland in Wisconson.

Determination of Wetland Losses and Gains

The Fish and Wildlife Service and the Natural Resources Conservation Service both collect data on wetland changes. Each agency has a different mission and different legislative mandates. Both agencies use the Cowardin *et al.* (1979) wetland definition in their respective inventories. For programmatic reasons, the Natural Resources Conservation Service also records data on wetlands as defined by the Food Security Act of 1985 (PL-99-198). The latter represents a subset of wetlands defined by the Cowardin *et al.* system. The process of identifying or attributing cause for wetland losses or gains has been investigated by both the Service and Natural Resources Conservation Service. During 1998 and 1999, the Natural Resources Conservation Service and the Service launched a concerted effort to develop a uniform system of definitions to attribute wetland losses and gains to their causes.

During April and May 1999, cooperative interagency field evaluations were conducted to field test the definitions used by the Service on its wetland status and trends plots to attribute wetland losses or gains. Field exercises involving the participation of up to four Federal agencies (Fish and Wildlife Service, Environmental Protection Agency, Office of Management and Budget and Natural Resources Conservation Service) were conducted in Florida, Louisiana and Minnesota. These exercises consisted of a careful review of determinations made on 89 sample plots. Field evaluation of these plots resulted in no disagreement among agency representatives with how the Service attributes wetland losses or gains.

The categories used to determine the cause of wetland losses and gains are described below.

Wapanocca National Wildlife Refuge, Arkansas.
(M. Caldwell)

Agriculture

The definition of agriculture follows Anderson *et al.* (1976) and includes land used primarily for the production of food and fiber. Agricultural activity may be shown by distinctive geometric field and road patterns on the landscape and/or by tracks produced by livestock or mechanized equipment. Examples of agricultural land uses include horticultural crops, row and close grown crops, hayland, pastureland, native pastures and range land, and farm infrastructures. Examples of what this study determined to be agricultural land uses are:

Horticultural crops are crops that include orchard fruits (apples, grapefruit, oranges, peaches, pears and like species). Also included are nuts such as almonds, pecans and walnuts; vineyards including grapes and hops; bush-fruit such as blueberries; berries such as strawberries or raspberries; and commercial flower growing and cutting operations.

Row and close-grown crops include field and sweet corn, sorghum, soybeans, cotton, peanuts, tobacco, sugar beets, potatoes, other truck vegetables including melons, beets, cabbage, cauliflower, pumpkins, tomatoes, sunflower and watermelon. Close-grown crops also include wheat, oats, barley, sod, ryegrass and similar graminoids.

Hayland and pastureland include grass, legumes, summer fallow, and grazed native grassland.

Other farmland includes farmsteads and ranch headquarters, commercial feedlots, greenhouses, hog facilities, nurseries and poultry facilities.

Forested Plantations

Forested plantations include areas of planted and managed forest stands. Planted pines, Christmas tree farms, clear cuts and other managed forest stands such as hardwood forestry, were included in this category.

Rural Development

Rural developments occur in sparse rural and suburban settings outside distinct urban cities and towns. They are characterized by non-intensive land use and sparse building density. Typically, a rural development is a cross-roads community that has a corner gas station and a convenience store which are surrounded by sparse residential housing and agriculture. Scattered suburban communities located outside of a major urban center can also be included in this category and some industrial and commercial complexes; isolated transportation, power, and communication facilities; strip mines; quarries; and recreational areas such as golf courses. Major highways through rural development areas were included in the rural development category.

Urban Development

Urban land consists of areas of intensive use in which much of the land is covered by structures (high building density). Urbanized areas are cities and towns that provide the goods and services needed to survive by modern day standards through a central business district. Services such as banking, medical and legal office buildings, supermarkets, and department stores make up the business center of a city. Commercial strip developments along main transportation routes, shopping centers, contiguous dense residential areas, industrial and commercial complexes, transportation, power and communication facilities, city parks, ball fields and golf courses were included in the urban category.

Other Land Uses

Other Land Use is composed of uplands not characterized by the previous categories. Typically these lands would include native prairie, unmanaged or non-patterned upland forests and scrub lands; and barren land. Lands in transition may also fit into this category.

A freshwater wetland along the Upper Mississippi River between Minnesota and Wisconsin. (U.S. Fish and Wildlife Service)

Results

Data for the 1986 to 1997 study period are presented in Appendix C, and they are summarized in Table 2.

National Status of Wetland Resources

An estimated 105.5 million acres (42.7 million ha) of wetlands remained in the conterminous United States in 1997. The coefficient of variation of the National estimate is 2.8 percent. Between 1986 and 1997, the estimated total net loss of wetlands was 644,000 acres (260,700 ha). The estimated annual rate of loss during this period was 58,500 acres (23,700 ha). The coefficient of variation of the loss rate is 36 percent (i.e., the estimated annual loss rate is

between 38,000 and 80,000 acres). The annual rate of loss has declined 80 percent since the period from the mid 1970s to the mid 1980s (Dahl and Johnson 1991).

Among the wetlands sampled, 55 percent were located in or adjacent to lands classified as other uplands. An additional 31 percent were in or adjacent to agricultural lands; 24 percent in or adjacent to silviculture; and 5 percent were in or adjacent to urban areas[1].

Ninety-five percent of the remaining wetlands were freshwater wetlands. Five percent were estuarine or marine wetlands (Figure 7). Among all freshwater wetlands, freshwater

---

[1] Percentages exceed 100 since some wetlands are adjacent to more than one upland type.

Figure 7 A–D. Wetland area (A) compared to total area of the conterminous United States; (B) percentage of estuarine and freshwater types; (C) estuarine cover types; (D) freshwater cover types.

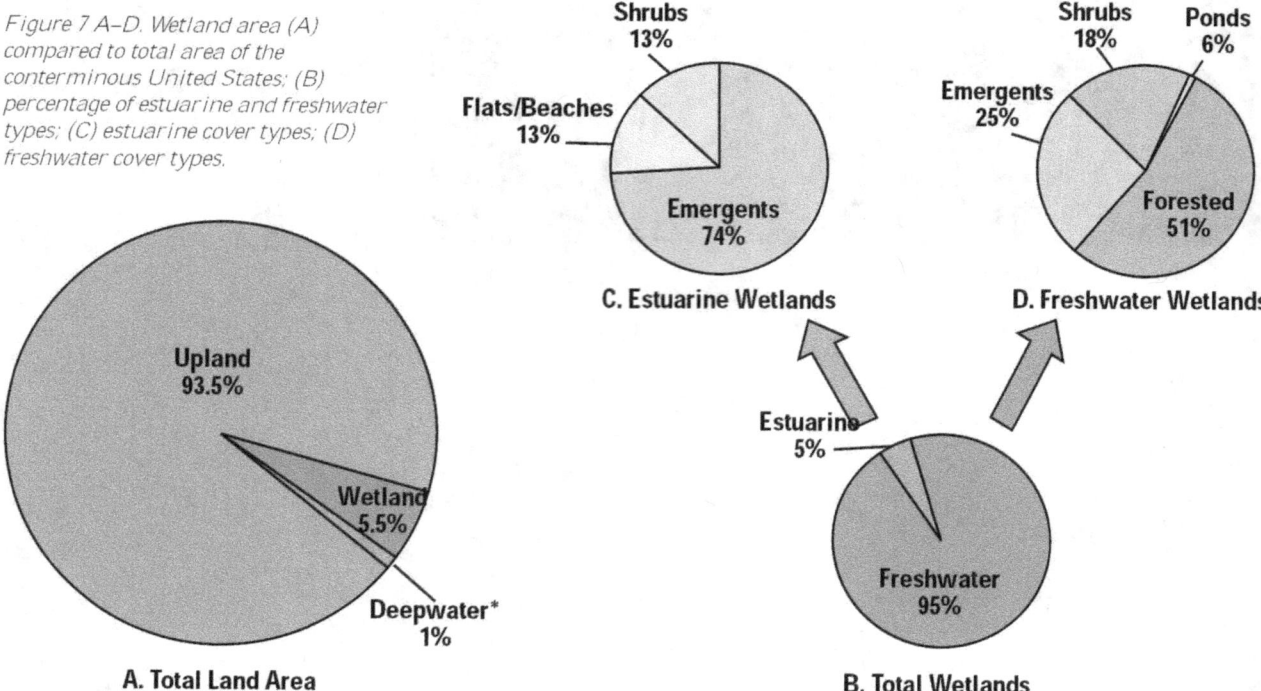

C. Estuarine Wetlands

- Shrubs 13%
- Flats/Beaches 13%
- Emergents 74%

D. Freshwater Wetlands

- Shrubs 18%
- Ponds 6%
- Emergents 25%
- Forested 51%

B. Total Wetlands

- Estuarine 5%
- Freshwater 95%

A. Total Land Area

- Upland 93.5%
- Wetland 5.5%
- Deepwater* 1%

*Excludes area of the Great Lakes

forested wetlands made up the single largest category (50.7 million acres or 20.5 million ha).

Attribution of Wetland Loss

Using the study definitions for the causes of wetland losses and gains, this study determined that urban development accounted for an estimated 30 percent of all wetland losses. Estimates for the other loss categories included 26 percent to agriculture, 23 percent to silviculture, and 21 percent to rural development. An estimated 98 percent of all wetlands converted to other uses were freshwater wetlands.

Table 2. Change in wetland area for selected wetland and deepwater categories, 1986 to 1997. The coefficient of variation (CV) for each entry (expressed as a percentage) is given in parentheses.

	Area in thousands of acres			
Wetland/Deepwater Category	Estimated area, 1986	Estimated area, 1997	Change, 1986–97	Change (in percent)
Marine Intertidal	133.1 (19.6)	130.9 (19.9)	–2.2 (88.5)	–1.7
Estuarine Intertidal Non-vegetated[1]	580.4 (10.7)	580.1 (10.6)	-0.3 (*)	–0.1
Estuarine Intertidal Vegetated[2]	4,623.1 (4.0)	4,615.2 (4.0)	-7.9 (75.1)	–0.2
All Intertidal Wetlands	5,336.6 (3.8)	5,326.2 (3.8)	–10.4 (73.0)	–0.2
Freshwater Non-vegetated[3]	5,251.0 (4.1)	5,914.3 (3.9)	663.3 (13.4)	12.6
Freshwater Vegetated[4]	95,548.1 (3.0)	94,251.2 (3.0)	–1,296.9 (17.1)	–1.4
Freshwater Emergent	26,383.3 (8.1)	25,157.1 (8.4)	–1,226.2 (18.2)	–4.6
Freshwater Forested	51,929.6 (2.8)	50,728.5 (2.8)	1,201.1 (23.8)	–2.3
Freshwater Shrub	17,235.2 (4.2)	18,365.6 (4.1)	1,130.4 (25.7)	6.6
All Freshwater Wetlands	100,799.1 (2.9)	100,165.5 (2.9)	633.6 (36.5)	–0.6
All Wetlands	106,135.7 (2.8)	105,491.7 (2.8)	–644.0 (36.0)	0.6
Deepwater Habitats				
Lacustrine[5]	14,608.9 (10.6)	14,725.3 (10.5)	116.4 (*)	0.8
Riverine	6,291.1 (9.6)	6,255.9 (9.4)	–35.2 (*)	–0.6
Estuarine Subtidal	17,637.6 (2.2)	17,663.9 (2.2)	26.3 (95.6)	0.1
All Deepwater Habitats	38,537.6 (4.4)	38,645.1 (4.4)	107.5 (*)	0.3
All Wetlands and Deepwater Habitats[1,2]	144,673.3 (2.4)	144,136.8 (2.4)	–536.5 (30.7)	–0.4

* Statistically unreliable

[1] Includes the categories: Estuarine Intertidal Aquatic Bed and Estuarine Intertidal Unconsolidated Shore.

[2] Includes the categories: Estuarine Intertidal Emergent and Estuarine Intertidal Shrub.

[3] Includes the categories: Palustrine Aquatic Bed, Palustrine Unconsolidated Bottom and Palustrine Unconsolidated Shore.

[4] Includes the categories: Palustrine Emergent, Palustrine Forested and Palustrine Shrub.

[5] Does not include the Great Lakes.

Intertidal Estuarine and Marine Wetlands

Intertidal wetlands include salt marshes and salt-tolerant shrubs; non-vegetated wetland such as sand bars, mud flats, and tidally exposed shoals; and shallow water components of the marine system such as sand beaches and shorelines. These wetlands were found in the low-lying coastal areas that are flooded periodically by tidal waters (Hefner *et al.* 1994). In 1997, there were an estimated 5.3 million acres (2.2 million ha) of marine and estuarine intertidal wetlands, that made up about 5 percent of the total wetland acreage in the conterminous United States.

Estuarine emergents (Figure 8) and estuarine shrub wetlands (Figure 9) made up 87 percent of the estuarine wetlands in the conterminous United States, totaling 4.6 million acres (1.9 million ha). Non-vegetated estuarine and marine wetlands, including beaches, flats, and shoals, comprised 13 percent of all intertidal wetlands or 711,000 acres (287,900 ha).

The changes that occurred between 1986 and 1997 in estuarine and marine wetlands are shown in Table 3. The largest acreage change was an estimated net loss of 14,500 acres (5,900 ha) of estuarine emergent wetlands. The greatest percent change was a decline of 1.7 percent of marine intertidal beaches. Estuarine and marine wetlands accounted for 2 percent of the overall wetland losses when all types were considered. During the study, estuarine and marine wetland losses totaled less than 1,000 acres (405 ha) annually. The major factor in estuarine and marine wetland loss

Figure 8. Estuarine emergents (salt marsh) near Edisto Island, South Carolina (1995).
(M. Caldwell)

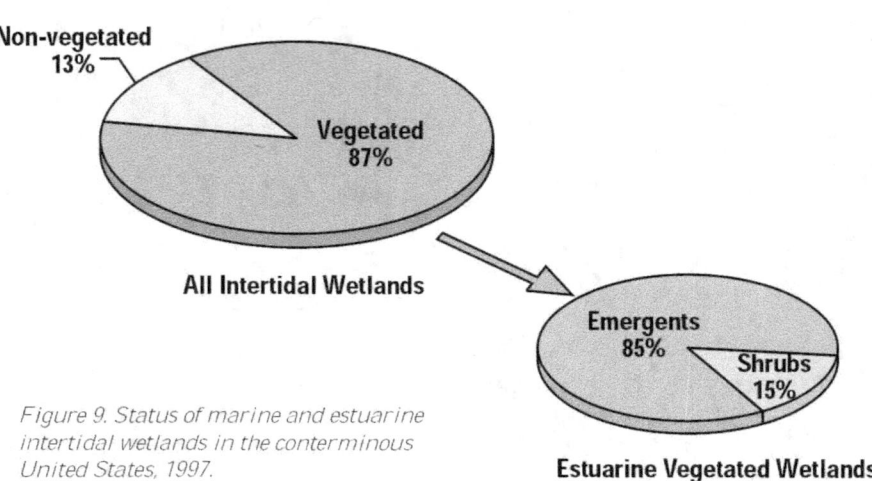

Figure 9. Status of marine and estuarine intertidal wetlands in the conterminous United States, 1997.

was development. Urban and rural development combined, accounted for 43 percent of the estuarine and marine wetland losses (Figure 10). Other upland land uses, which involved fill or spoil deposition, accounted for 30 percent of the loss. The total and annual change in estuarine and marine wetland types is shown in Table 4.

Seventy five percent of all estuarine and marine losses were in emergent salt marsh wetlands. The emergent salt marsh wetlands of the Atlantic and Gulf coast states experienced losses due to development as well as saltwater inundation. The distribution of these emergent salt marsh wetlands is shown in Figure 11.

Emergent salt marsh wetlands typically occupy broad expanses of coastal lowlands. The mean size of salt marsh wetlands on the study

plots was 44 acres (18 ha). Overall, the study revealed that estuarine wetlands in urban settings were fairly rare. Approximately 4.8 percent of estuarine salt marsh wetlands were adjacent to or within urban areas. The mean size of other estuarine wetland types was smaller; estuarine shrub wetlands sampled were 16 acres (7 ha) and estuarine bars, flats and shoals were 12 acres (5 ha).

Figure 10. Percent of estuarine and marine wetlands lost to freshwater wetlands, deepwater, or upland categories between 1986 and 1997.

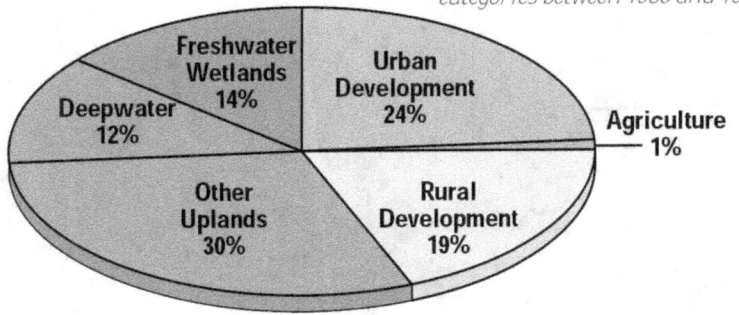

Table 3. Estuarine and marine intertidal wetland area and change, 1986 to 1997. The coefficient of variation (CV) for each entry (expressed as a percentage) is given in parentheses.

Wetland Category	Area in thousands of acres			
	Estimated area, 1986	Estimated area, 1997	Gain or loss, 1986–97	Area (as percent) of all intertidal wetland, 1997
Marine Intertidal	133.1 (19.6)	130.9 (19.9)	−2.2 (88.5)	2.5
Estuarine Unconsolidated Shore	551.3 (10.9)	550.8 (10.8)	−0.5 (*)	10.3
Estuarine Aquatic Bed	29.1 (27.1)	29.3 (26.9)	0.2 (*)	0.6
Marine and Estuarine Intertidal Non-vegetated[1]	580.4 (10.7)	580.1 (10.6)	−0.3 (*)	13.4
Estuarine Emergent	3,956.9 (4.1)	3,942.4 (4.1)	−14.5 (49.2)	74.0
Estuarine Shrub	666.2 (12.6)	672.8 (12.6)	6.6 (76.5)	12.6
Estuarine Intertidal Vegetated[2]	4,623.1 (4.0)	4,615.2 (4.0)	−7.9 (75.1)	86.6
Changes in coastal deepwater area, 1986–97				
Estuarine Subtidal	17,637.6 (2.2)	17,663.9 (2.2)	26.3 (95.6)	—

* Statistically unreliable.

[1] Includes the categories: Estuarine Unconsolidated Shore and Estuarine Aquatic Bed.

[2] Includes the categories: Estuarine Emergent and Estuarine Shrub.

	Sparse
	Moderate
	Dense
	Insufficient data

Figure 11. Distribution of estuarine emergents (salt marsh) along the Atlantic and Gulf coasts, 1997. Sparse distribution is less than or equal to 5 percent areal coverage of coastal quadrangles; moderate is 6–20 percent; and dense is greater than 20 percent areal coverage.

Table 4. Estuarine and marine intertidal wetland losses, 1986 to 1997. The coefficient of variation (CV) for each entry (expressed as a percentage) is given in parentheses.

Wetland Type	Area lost, 1986–97 (acres)	Annual change (acres)	Losses as percent of annual intertidal change
Estuarine Vegetated Wetlands[1]	−7,830 (75)	−712 (*)	75
Estuarine and Marine, Non-Vegetated[2]	−2,590 (*)	−236 (*)	25
Total Estuarine and Marine Wetland	−10,420 (73)	−948 (*)	100

[1] Includes estuarine emergents and estuarine shrub categories.

[2] Includes estuarine unconsolidated shore, estuarine aquatic bed, and marine intertidal categories.

*Statistically unreliable.

Freshwater Wetlands

Freshwater, or palustrine, wetlands occur in every State. They include forested wetlands, freshwater emergent marshes, shrub wetlands, and freshwater ponds less than 20 acres (8 ha).

An estimated 100.2 million acres (40.6 million ha) of freshwater wetlands of various types remained in the conterminous United States in 1997. There were 50.7 million acres (20.5 million ha) of forested wetlands, 25.2 million acres (10.2 million ha) of freshwater emergents, and 18.4 million acres (7.5 million ha) of freshwater shrub wetlands. There were also an estimated 5.5 million acres (2.2 million ha) of freshwater ponds. The distribution of freshwater wetland types is shown in Figure 12.

From 1986 to 1997, both freshwater forested wetlands and freshwater emergent marshes experienced substantial losses of 1.2 million acres (486,000 ha) from each category. These losses in wetland area were somewhat offset by gains in freshwater shrub wetlands (1.1 million acres or 445,000 ha) and freshwater ponds (631,000 acres or 256,000 ha). The estimated net loss of all freshwater wetland types was 633,600 acres (256,500 ha) during the period of this study. This indicates that 98 percent of all wetland losses in the conterminous United States between 1986 and 1997 were to freshwater wetlands.

The mean size of freshwater wetlands sampled indicated that freshwater forested wetlands were the largest type (Table 5). The mean size for forested wetlands was 21 acres (9 ha). Freshwater shrub and emergent wetlands were 8 acres (3.2 ha) and 7 acres (2.8 ha), respectively. The mean size of freshwater ponds was 1–2 acres (0.4–0.8 ha).

Freshwater Lakes and Reservoirs

Deepwater lakes and reservoirs showed a modest increase, with a net gain of 116,400 acres (47,100 ha). The rate of lake and reservoir creation declined 43 percent from the 1970s to 1980s. The reason for this decline is not known.

Table 5. Mean size and range of freshwater wetlands as they appeared within the sample units in 1997.

Freshwater Wetland Category	Mean size (acres)	Range (acres)[1]
Freshwater forest	21	<1 to 2,560
Freshwater shrub	8	<1 to 2,416
Freshwater emergent	7	<1 to 2,560
Freshwater ponds	1–2	<1 to 1,000[2]
Other Freshwater types	3–4	<1 to 700

[1] The upper limit is restricted by the sample plot size and cannot be determined.

[2] The upper limit reflects the area of ponds connected in series.

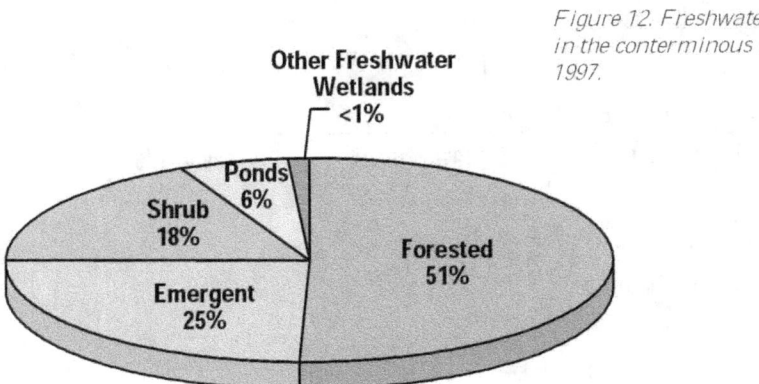

Figure 12. Freshwater wetland types in the conterminous United States, 1997.

Discussion

Dahl and Johnson (1991) estimated that 103.2 million acres (41.8 million ha) of wetlands existed in the conterminous United States in 1984. This study produced a revised 1986 estimate of 106.1 million acres (43 million ha). The adjusted estimate of wetland area for the mid 1980s was within the statistical range of both the 1991 study and this report. Other factors contributing to this adjustment were corrections to the wetland data set, and improved data capture and measurement techniques.

This study estimated that 105.5 million acres (42.7 million ha) of wetlands were in the conterminous United States at the end of 1997. Between 1986 and 1997, a net of 644,000 acres (260,700 ha) of wetlands were lost. The wetland loss rate in the United States continued to decline. The average annual rate of wetland loss decreased by 80 percent compared with the rate in the previous decades (Figure 13). Several factors contributed to this substantial decline in the loss rate. Important among them were the application and enforcement of wetland protection measures, elimination of some incentives for wetland drainage, public education and outreach about the value and functions of wetlands, private land initiatives, coastal monitoring and protection programs, natural restoration due to hydrologic cycles, and wetland restoration and creation actions undertaken by society.

Figure 13. Average annual net wetland loss over time for the conterminous United States. (Sources: Frayer et al. 1983; Dahl and Johnson 1991; this study.)

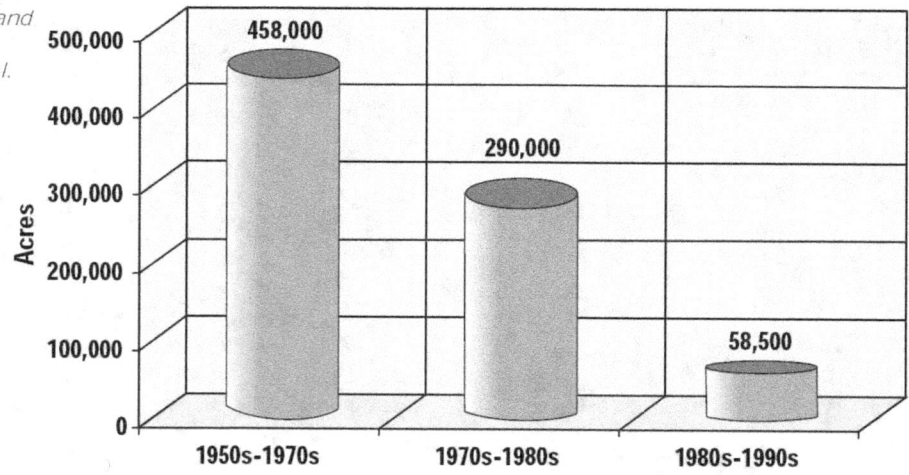

Estuarine and Marine Wetland Resources

Saltwater intertidal wetlands are dynamic areas of economic and social importance. These wetlands provide valuable nursery, feeding, breeding, staging and resting areas for many fishes, shellfish, mammals and birds. Nearly 45 percent of the Nation's endangered and threatened species are dependent on coastal habitats (U.S. Fish and Wildlife Service 1995). Many species of shorebirds use exposed estuarine bars and flats as feeding and resting areas. Wading birds use shallow water salt marshes and tidal pools for foraging. Endangered sea turtles nest along estuarine and marine beaches and sand spits. Near shore vegetated wetlands provide habitat for estuarine fish species. Formation of shallow water oyster beds is tracked closely as an indicator of water quality conditions and their importance to commercial fisheries.

Three major categories of estuarine and marine wetlands were included in this study: estuarine intertidal emergents (salt and brackish water marshes), estuarine shrubs (mangroves and other salt tolerant woody species), and estuarine and marine intertidal non-vegetated wetlands (beaches, tidal flats, shoals, sand spits and bars). A fourth category includes the seagrasses and submerged aquatic vegetation. Because of their importance to fish and wildlife, a brief discussion of seagrasses and submerged aquatic vegetation is included in the special inset section (next page).

Between 1986 and 1997 there was an estimated net loss of 10,400 acres (4,200 ha) of estuarine and marine wetlands. The rate of decline for these wetlands was reduced more than 82 percent since the previous decade (Dahl and Johnson 1991). Enactment of legislation such as the Coastal Wetlands Planning, Protection, and Restoration Act, combined with other Federal and State conservation efforts contributed to this reduction in estuarine and marine wetland losses.

Saltwater intrusion, or the loss of wetland to open saltwater systems, due to natural and man-induced activities, accounted for 12 percent of the estuarine and marine wetland losses. The areas along the Gulf coast where estuarine wetlands were lost to deepwater during this study are shown in Figure 14. Barras *et al.* (1994) showed that land loss to open water is a continuing problem in certain watersheds along the Louisiana coast.

Urban and rural development activities, and the conversion of wetlands to other upland land uses, accounted for most of the estuarine and marine wetland losses between 1986 and 1997. Areas where urban expansion and rural development resulted in estuarine wetland losses are shown in Figure 15.

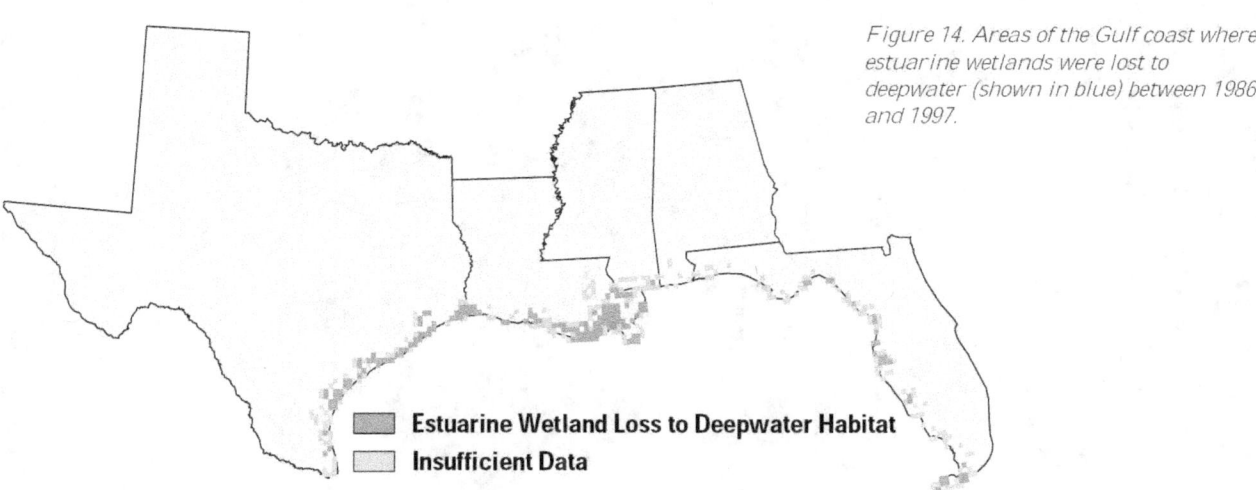

Figure 14. Areas of the Gulf coast where estuarine wetlands were lost to deepwater (shown in blue) between 1986 and 1997.

■ **Estuarine Wetland Loss to Deepwater Habitat**
□ **Insufficient Data**

Seagrasses and Submerged Aquatic Vegetation

Seagrasses or submerged aquatic vegetation are plants that are adapted to living in shallow, subtidal estuarine or marine environments. Seagrasses provide important environmental functions including stabilizing sediments and adjacent shorelines, serving as nursery areas for many fish and shellfish, playing an important role in nutrient cycling, and providing cover or habitat for sessile and mobile fauna (Thayer *et al.* 1984). Seagrasses may also be directly consumed by geese, dugongs, manatees, and sea turtles (Zieman 1982; Lanyon *et al.* 1989).

Seagrasses occur in every coastal State except South Carolina and Georgia (Fonseca *et al.* 1998), but there is no comprehensive national data on the status of seagrass abundance or recent trends. The National Oceanic and Atmospheric Administration (NOAA) is working to fill some of the data gaps on seagrass habitat trends.

Mapping seagrasses poses challenges beyond mapping other wetlands. In order to penetrate the water column NOAA employs conventional color photography acquired under specific environmental conditions. Proper tidal stage, sea state, etc., are crucial to capturing all of the resource present. Additional technologies such as videography and acoustics are often necessary for a successful mapping and monitoring effort.

Changes in Aquatic Vegetation Beds

These wetlands are subject to rapid change coincident with stressors such as dredging and filling, abnormal water temperature changes, input of chemical wastes, increased turbidity and development of adjacent uplands and wetlands (Thayer *et al.* 1984; Ferguson *et al.* 1993).

Information on seagrass distribution helps state and local officials with permitting, waterfront planning, and research needs. Comparing maps of the same area from different years helps managers monitor the health of this resource .

Changes to seagrass beds in the Cape Lookout, North Carolina, region between 1985 and 1988. For this figure, the change data were superimposed on a conventional aerial photograph taken in 1988. This photograph represents an area approximately five-by-five miles. In addition to aerial photography, towed and hand-held underwater videography is used as a verification tool. Single-beam acoustics are used in deeper, more turbid areas. The acoustic sensor tool also takes bathymetric readings. (National Oceanic and Atmospheric Administration)

Areas of no seagrass change

Areas of seagrass loss

Areas of seagrass gain

Figure 15. Areas along the Gulf and Atlantic coasts where estuarine wetlands were lost to urban or rural development (shown in orange) between 1986 and 1997.

■ **Estuarine Wetland Loss to Urban or Rural Development**

■ **Insufficient Data**

Figure 16. The broad coastal plain of the southeastern Atlantic supports expansive estuarine wetlands (Coastal South Carolina, 1996). (M. Caldwell)

37

Estuarine Emergent Wetlands

The coastlines of New England and the Pacific Northwest are typified by high energy, rocky headlands punctuated by small estuarine wetlands, which are mostly restricted to protected embayments (Chabreck 1988; Ardito and Finch 1998). In contrast, the broad coastal plain of the southeastern Atlantic and Gulf States supports much more expansive areas of estuarine wetlands, particularly emergent salt marsh (Figure 16). Most of the changes in the estuarine wetlands occurred in the southern coastal States from Virginia to Texas.

Estuarine emergents declined by an estimated 14,450 acres (5,850 ha) between 1986 and 1997, a 0.4 percent loss. Most of this wetland loss (58 percent) was caused by open water intrusion from undetermined circumstances. Of the estuarine emergent losses recorded, 58 percent were lost to open saltwater, 34 percent to uplands, and 8 percent were converted to other estuarine types, primarily shrubs. Sea level rise, marshland sloughing into deeper water bays and sounds, and land subsidence may have contributed to these losses. The processes that cause saltwater intrusion, whether natural or human-induced, are complex, and not well understood (Sallenger and Williams 1989). Estuarine marshes in coastal Louisiana have experienced these kinds of stressors over the past several decades (Britsch and Dunbar 1993). In places such as Louisiana and the upper Texas Gulf coast, these phenomena influenced wetland losses in habitats other than in the estuarine system (White and Tremblay 1994). Examples of non-estuarine wetland types in coastal drainages subject to saltwater intrusion included tidally-influenced freshwater marshes and forested or shrub swamps.

The effects of saltwater intrusion are also seen to a lesser extent on areas of the Atlantic coast. In Virginia and North Carolina, some areas were inundated with enough saltwater to establish estuarine emergents. This was observed on several small tracts of farmland and in several freshwater wetlands.

Although estuarine salt marsh wetlands are among the most ecologically productive natural resources in the United States, about 5,000 acres (2,020 ha) of estuarine salt marsh wetlands were filled and developed from 1986 to 1997. Urban and rural development of houses, roads, and infrastructure accounted for about 2,300 acres (930 ha) of these losses (Figures 17 and 18). Other upland land uses in rural areas filled another 2,700 acres (1,090 ha). Fill accounted for 34 percent of the losses in the estuarine emergent wetland category. Development pressure on wetlands remains intense along the Gulf and Atlantic coasts (Figure 19). Many Federal agencies are involved in the regulation, protection, and monitoring of estuarine wetlands, coastal areas, and the species that inhabit them. Many coastal States also have established coastal zone management plans, growth management plans, and coastal resource agencies.

A ditched area in the Atlantic coastal plain.

A.

Figure 17. Two examples of development in coastal areas. A) A highway project resulted in placement of fill in estuarine emergent wetlands in coastal Georgia, 1995, and B) an estuarine emergent marsh was filled for a new development in coastal Texas.
(B, U.S. Fish and Wildlife Service: J. Dick)

B.

Figure 18. Development along Florida's Gulf coast beaches.

Estuarine Shrubs

Estuarine wetlands face a dual threat from natural stressors such as storms, wind and wave erosion, land subsidence, sea level rise and stressors caused by population increases in many coastal counties. These interactions were apparent in an examination of the estuarine shrub wetland trends. The data indicate that estuarine shrub wetlands increased by 6,600 acres (2,670 ha) during 1986 to 1997.

The increase in area was from conversion of other estuarine wetland types, predominantly estuarine emergents and estuarine flats. The data indicate that estuarine shrubs increased by a much greater amount (gross change approaches 17,000 acres or 6,900 ha), because of conversions from estuarine emergents and estuarine bars and flats. The gross increase was tempered by coastal changes as estuarine shrubs died back in some areas and were replaced by emergents, were scoured and removed by shifting sediments, or became inundated by coastal waters. These changes occurred throughout the estuarine and marine systems, and they can be attributed to natural influences such as storms, wind and wave erosion. Of the nearly 17,000 acres of estuarine shrub wetlands, 7,650 acres (3,100 ha) or 45 percent were converted to other estuarine and marine wetlands and coastal waters. Another 39 percent remained as estuarine shrub wetlands, and the remaining 14 percent (2450 acres or 990 ha) was lost to some form of development. Urban and rural development accounted for about 1,800 acres (720 ha) of these losses (Figure 20). Other forms of development, including some freshwater ponds built as water traps for seaside golf courses, accounted for the remaining 650 acres (260 ha) of loss. These losses were masked by the conversion of enough other coastal wetland types to estuarine shrubs to yield a net gain for this wetland type.

Estuarine shrub wetlands are geographically restricted to the south Atlantic and Gulf coasts; most are in southern Florida where they are dominated by mangroves (**Rhizophora mangle**, *Avicennia germinans, Laguncularia racemosa*). This was an important consideration because the increased extent of estuarine shrub wetlands may have resulted from the increased occurrence of salt tolerant invasive species. Brazilian pepper (*Schinus terebinthifolius*) is an aggressive woody shrub originally from South American that is now found throughout south and central Florida. Brazilian pepper can survive hydrologic conditions ranging from coastal mangrove

Figure 19. Coastal developments encroach on estuarine shrub wetlands (mangroves) along the Intracoastal Waterway in Florida.

wetlands to inland pine forests (McCann *et al.* 1996). Because this shrub can out compete native plants, including mangroves growing along the edges of estuaries, it is becoming harder to differentiate the estuarine shrub boundary in those areas where Brazilian pepper extends from the estuary to the uplands. There may be as many as 700,000 acres (283,400 ha) of Brazilian pepper in Florida (Florida Dept. of Environmental Protection 1994).

Beaches, Bars, Flats, and Shoals

The non-vegetated estuarine wetlands include beaches, bars, flats, and shoals, and a narrow strip of marine sand beaches. These wetlands experience many influences including coastal storms, erosion, and deposition resulting from wave action, inundation from sea level rise, and artificial manipulation.

Sand and mud flats are found where sediments accumulate, and they are often associated with coastal embayments, spits, barrier islands, or estuaries (Figure 20). Although these areas are not vegetated, they are important habitat for fishes and shellfish including eastern oysters (*Crassostrea virginica*), mussels, clams, crabs and grass and sand shrimp. These organisms in turn, attract shorebirds and wading birds (Whitlatch 1982).

The constant movement of sediment and water resulting from tidal influences, wave action and coastal storms, makes these wetlands dynamic. Beaches and shorelines erode, sandbars and shoals form or disappear, sand spits elongate, and barrier islands change shape or disappear (Frankenberg 1995). These changes were the result of coastal processes manifested in dramatic fashion with the movement of entire barrier islands (Figure 21A–C) and were responsible for about 25 percent of all estuarine and marine wetland losses observed during this study. From 1986 to 1997, loss of estuarine non-vegetated wetlands (flats, bars, and shoals) was not statistically significant (less than 1 percent of all estuarine wetland losses). However, loss of marine non-vegetated wetlands (primarily beaches and seaward shoreline features) accounted for 2,590 acres (1,050 ha). Coastal erosion and inundation were the primary reasons for the majority (73 percent) of these losses.

The areas of the coastline that exhibited the most noticeable change in marine non-vegetated wetland resources include the southern Atlantic coast and Florida Bay.

Figure 20. Tidal flats along an estuarine spit in Walkalla County, Florida (1993).

Figure 21 A–C. Color infrared aerial photographs showing changes to coastal features between (A) 1989; (B) 1994; and (C) 1999. Vegetated wetlands appearing as mottled green or blue remain fairly constant while non-vegetated spits and bars show the result of coastal influences (Georgetown, South Carolina). Tide stage, sun angle and photographic emulsion may influence feature definition. (National Aerial Photography Program)

A. 1989

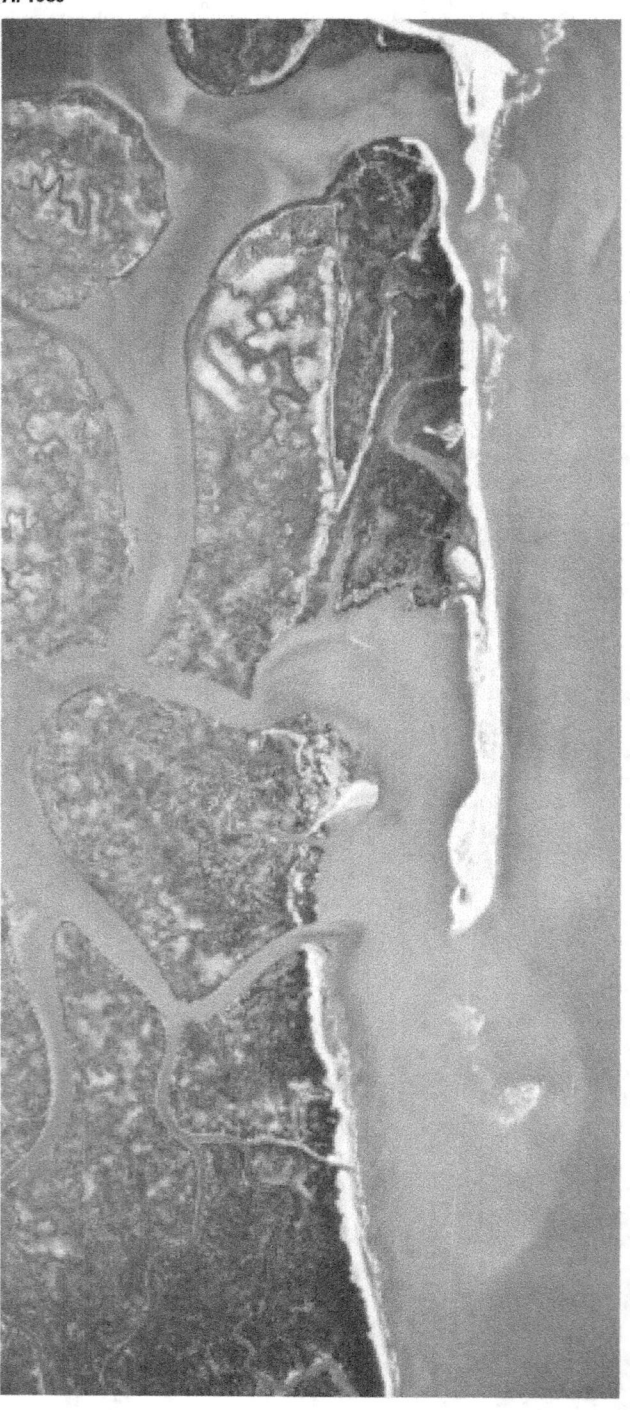

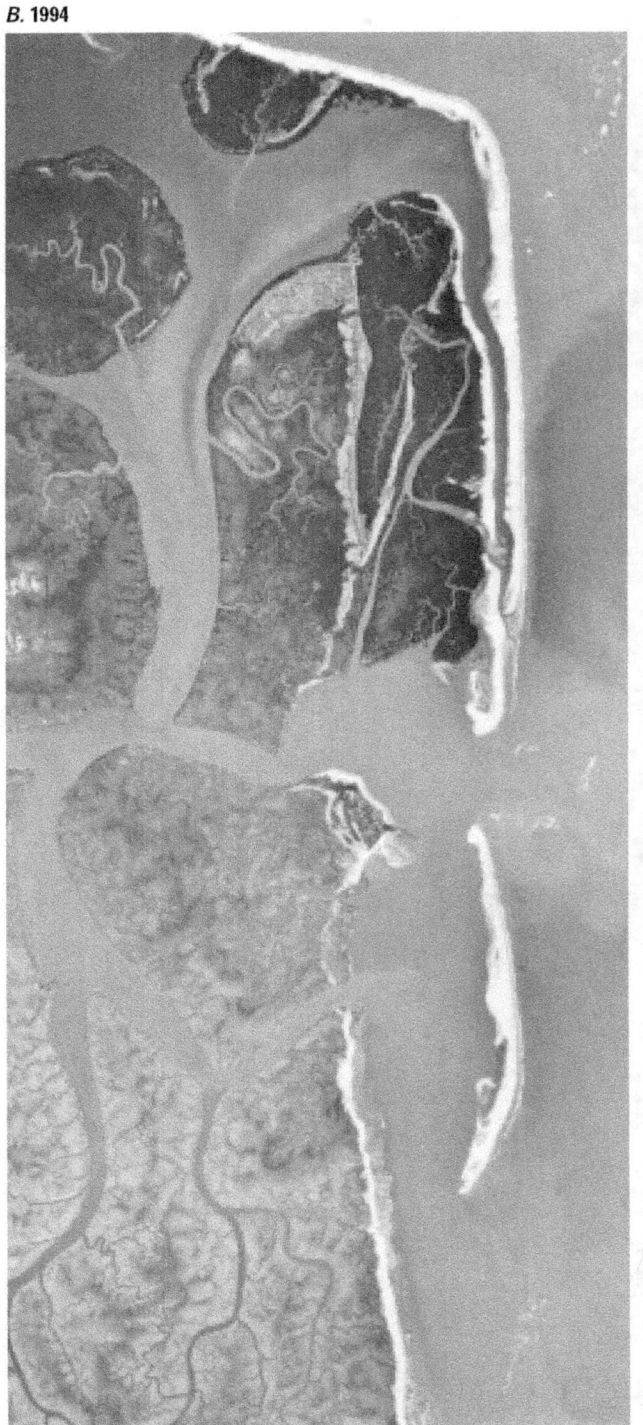

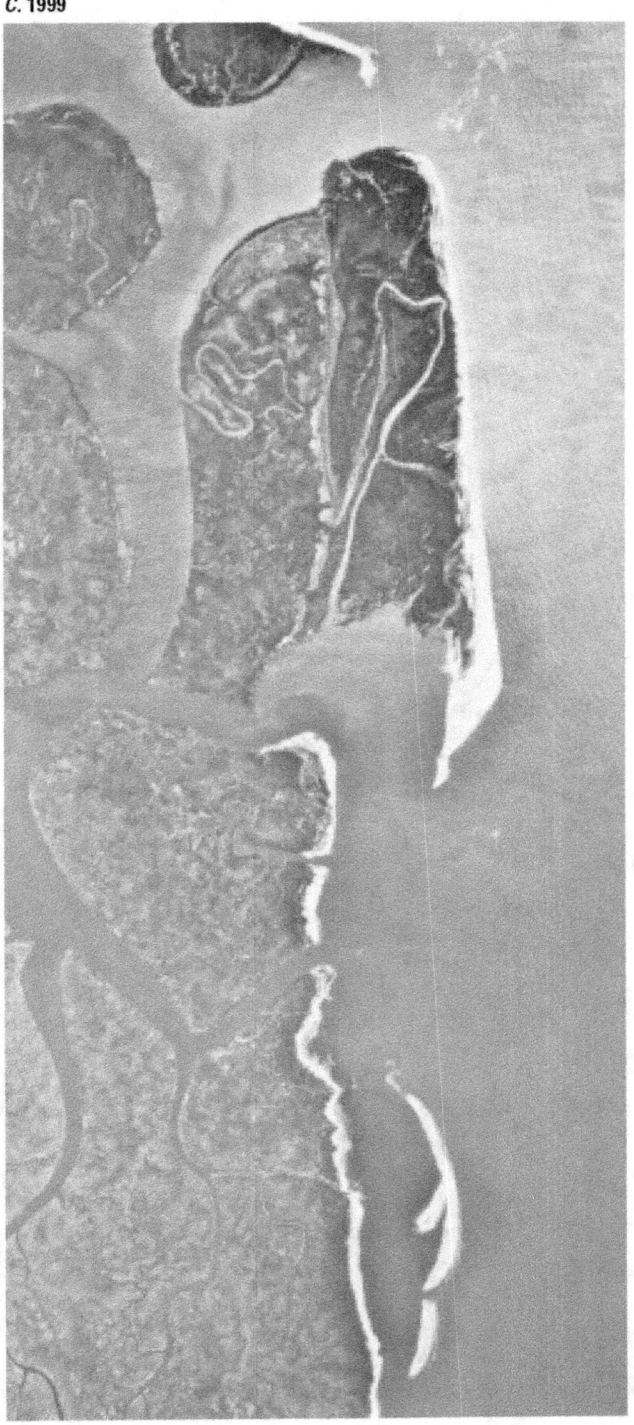

Long-term Trends in Estuarine Wetland Types

Long-term trends in estuarine wetlands are shown in Figure 22A–C. The areal extent of estuarine intertidal wetland continued to decline through 1997, although the rate of decline slowed considerably from earlier periods (Frayer *et al.* 1983; Dahl and Johnson 1991). The areal extent of estuarine vegetated wetland declined, but the area of non-vegetated wetland types remained constant.

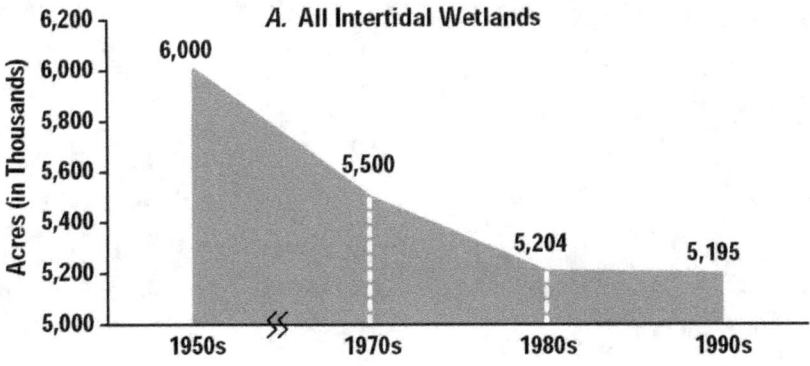

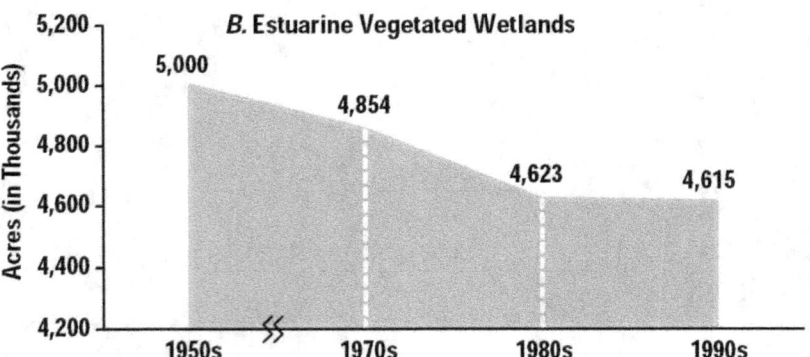

Figure 22 A–C. Long-term trends in (A) all estuarine intertidal wetlands; (B) estuarine vegetated wetlands; (C) estuarine non-vegetated wetlands, 1950s to 1997. (Source: Frayer et al. 1983; Dahl and Johnson 1991; this study.)

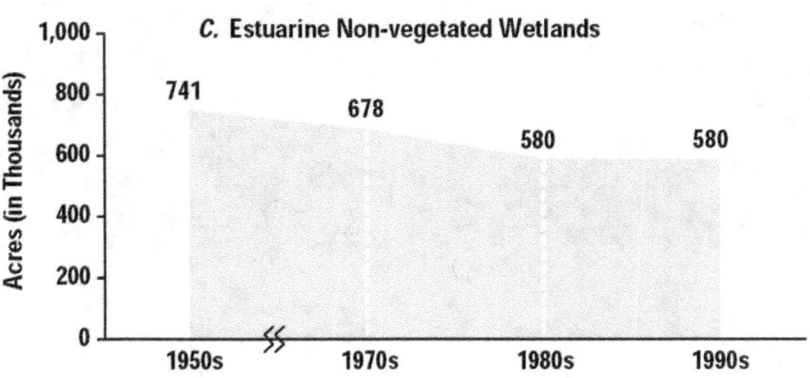

Freshwater Wetland Resources

Ninety-eight percent of all losses (633,600 acres; 256,500 ha) between 1986 and 1997 were to freshwater wetlands. Freshwater forested wetlands and freshwater emergent wetlands declined 2.3 percent and 4.6 percent, respectively. Some of these changes were due to conversion from forested or emergent wetland to shrub wetlands, which gained 6.6 percent during the same time period (Table 6). The numerical loss in wetland area was masked by a substantial gain in freshwater ponds (13 percent), although these were not equivalent habitat types.

Most freshwater wetland losses were from actions that changed them to some form of upland land use. Lands classified as urban accounted for 30 percent of the losses; agriculture 26 percent; upland silviculture 23 percent; and rural development 21 percent (Figure 23). Freshwater wetlands gained about 180,000 acres (72,900 ha) from the "other" lands category, primarily from construction of freshwater ponds and wetland restoration or creation on lands formerly classified as other uplands.

Forty percent of all freshwater wetlands sampled were located in or adjacent to agricultural lands (Figure 24). These wetlands are potentially affected by agricultural land use practices such as herbicide and pesticide applications, irrigation, livestock watering and waste, soil erosion and deposition.

The rate of freshwater wetland loss to agricultural activities declined substantially from the previous decade. Between the mid 1970s and 1984 about 1.0 million acres (404,900 ha) were lost to agriculture (Dahl and Johnson 1991), compared to 198,000 acres (80,200 ha) lost during this study. Implementation of the "Swampbuster" provisions of the 1985 Food Security Act (and its subsequent versions) and agricultural set-aside and land retirement programs are most likely responsible for the reduction in wetland losses.

Between 1986 and 1997, more freshwater emergent wetlands were lost to agriculture than either shrub or forested wetlands. During the previous decade, three times the number of shrub and forested wetlands than freshwater emergent wetlands were cut and drained for agricultural land (Dahl and Johnson 1991). This difference suggests that during the 1990s there was a decline in the number of forested wetlands converted to crop production. This helped reduce forested wetland losses in regions like the lower Mississippi alluvial plain and the bottomland hardwood wetlands of the southeast. The emergent wetlands that continue to be lost are geographically scattered and generally small wetlands; some were already partially drained by surface ditches or completely eliminated through intensified use of existing farmland. Practices such as the improvement of on-farm drainage, ditch clean-outs, or the elimination of partially drained wetlands were permitted under the various Food Security Act revisions. Bernert *et al.* (1999) observed this trend in the Willamette Valley, Oregon, and

---

Table 6. Freshwater wetland area and change, 1986 to 1997. The coefficient of variation (CV) for each entry (expressed as a percentage) is given in parentheses.

Wetland Category	Area in thousands of acres			Change (in percent)
	Estimated area, 1986	Estimated area, 1997	Change, 1986–97	
Freshwater Emergent	26,383.3 (8.1)	25,157.1 (8.4)	−1,226.2 (18.2)	−4.6
Freshwater Forested	51,929.6 (2.8)	50,728.5 (2.8)	−1,201.1 (23.8)	−2.3
Freshwater Shrub	17,235.2 (4.2)	18,365.6 (4.1)	1,130.4 (25.7)	6.6
Freshwater Vegetated Wetlands	95,548.1 (3.0)	94,251.2 (3.0)	−1,296.9 (17.1)	−1.4
Ponds*	4,868.8 (4.3)	5,500.1 (4.0)	631.3 (23.4)	13.0
Miscellaneous Types	382.2 (15.9)	414.2 (15.5)	32.0 (69.8)	8.4
Freshwater Non-vegetated	5,251.0 (4.1)	5,914.3 (3.9)	663.3 (13.4)	12.6
All Freshwater Wetlands	100,799.1 (2.9)	100,165.5 (2.9)	−633.6 (36.5)	-0.6

* Includes the categories: Palustrine Aquatic Bed and Palustrine Unconsolidated Bottom.

questioned the effectiveness of current agricultural policy to deal with wetland loss from intensified use of existing farmland.

Five percent of the freshwater wetlands sampled were located in or adjacent to urban centers and towns. Another 12 percent of freshwater wetlands were in or adjacent to areas classified as rural development.

Collectively, 51 percent or 383,300 acres (155,200 ha) of all the freshwater wetlands lost to uplands resulted from urban and rural development. Construction of buildings, roads, bridges or infrastructure in wetlands accounted for these losses. An example of how wetlands were lost to development projects is shown in Figures 25A–B.

Several scenarios could account for wetland losses from development. These involve permitted actions under Sections 10 and 404 of the Clean Water Act and after-the-fact permits, development allowed under general permit conditions, situations involving non-jurisdictional wetland

Figure 23. Change in wetlands converted to various land uses between 1986 and 1997.

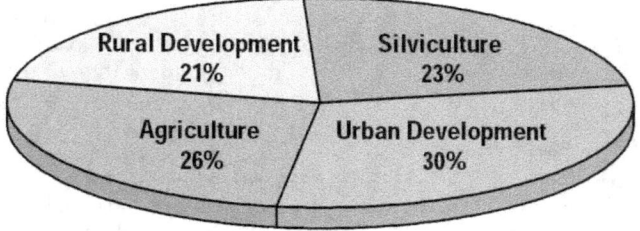

Rural Development 21%

Silviculture 23%

Agriculture 26%

Urban Development 30%

1989

Figure 25. Color infrared aerial photographs taken in 1989 and 1999 show development(s) proceeding in South Carolina. Changes to wetlands that have occurred include the loss of forested and shrub wetlands to upland; the conversion of forested and emeregent wetlands to open-water impoundments; loss of open water to upland; and the conversion of open water to emergent wetland. (National Aerial Photography Program)

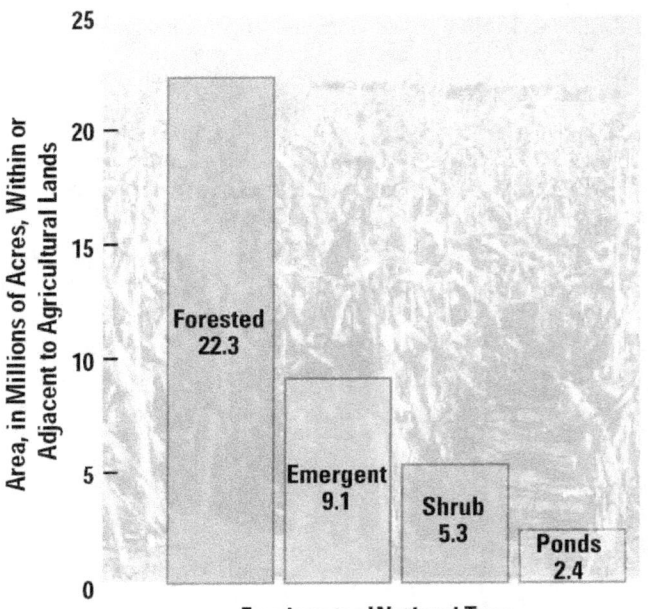

Figure 24. Freshwater wetlands, by type, that are within or adjacent to agricultural lands, 1997. (Photograph: E. Ciganovich)

1999

determinations, exemptions, or illegal activities that are subsequently detected and penalties assessed. The area of wetland loss from urban and rural development (383,300 acres or 155,200 ha) could have been ameliorated by gains in freshwater ponds and lakes (747,700 acres or 302,700 ha).

Freshwater non-tidal wetlands experienced the greatest development pressure just inland from the coastlines of the United States. Wetlands located in coastal watersheds of many coastal counties are undergoing rapid growth and they lead in many demographic indicators of development (Culliton 1998). These freshwater wetlands were most susceptible to development from rapid population growth and the demand for housing, transportation infrastructure, and commercial and recreational facilities (Good *et al.* 1997). The coastal counties where there were wetland losses between 1986 and 1997 are shown in Figure 26.

Low
Medium
High

Figure 26. Gulf and Atlantic coastal counties that experienced wetland losses to uplands between 1986 and 1997. Low level of loss indicates less that 20 acres, medium indicates 20–150 acres, and a high level of loss indicates greater than 150 acres of wetland lost.

Freshwater Forested Wetlands

There was more area of freshwater forested wetlands in the United States (50.7 million acres or 20.5 million ha) than any other wetland type. More than 1.2 million acres (485,800 ha) of forested wetlands were lost between 1986 and 1997. This was the result of the removal of 4 million acres (1.6 million ha) of forested wetland from the landscape and the conversion of 2.8 million acres (1.1 million ha), primarily shrubs, returning to the forested wetland category (Figure 27). Of the 4 million acres that underwent some change, most were converted to freshwater shrub wetlands by timber harvesting or other processes that removed the forested canopy but retained the wetland character. Although these areas remain as wetland, the removal of the forest canopy can be a radical alteration of the landscape resulting in changes in hydrology and wildlife value (Figure 28).

The loss rate of forested wetlands declined from 6.2 percent in the 1970s to the 1980s (Dahl and Johnson 1991), to 2.3 percent in this study. Of the forested wetlands lost to upland land uses, urban and rural development (Figure 29) accounted for the largest amount of the loss. Thirty-three percent or 148,400 acres (60,100 ha) were lost to urban and rural development. Another 139,100 acres (56,300 ha) were

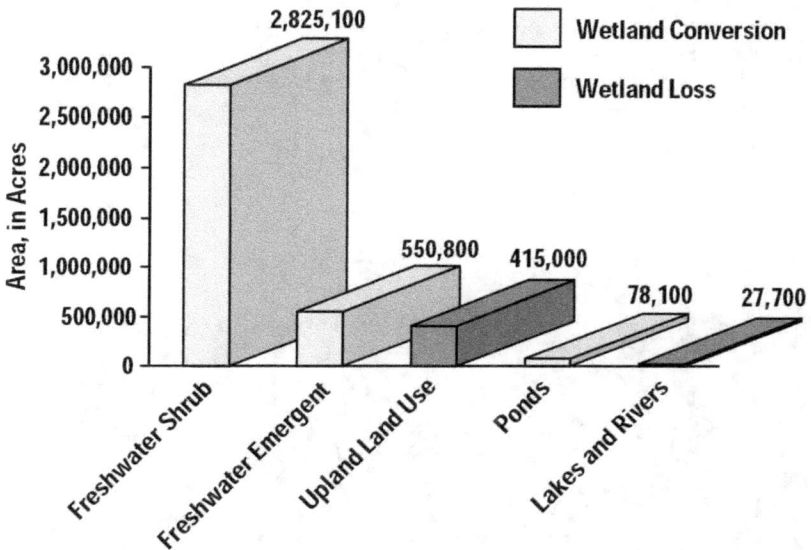

Figure 27. Cumulative loss and conversion of freshwater forested wetlands, 1986 to 1997.

Figure 28. A clear-cut of a former freshwater forested wetland in Oklahoma, 2000. This area represented a conversion within wetland categories from forest to emergent cover types without a change in area. (U.S. Fish and Wildlife Service: J. Dick)

49

classified as upland agriculture, whereas 23.8 percent or 107,000 acres (43,300 ha) were converted to managed forested plantations. Unidentified land uses were responsible for 12 percent (53,400 acres or 21,600 ha) of the forested wetland losses.

An additional 78,100 acres (31,600 ha) of forested wetlands were converted to freshwater ponds. Conversions to deepwater lakes resulted from human activities by either creation of new impoundments or by raising the water levels on existing impoundments and thus killing the trees (Tansey and Cost 1990). Floods, such as those along the Mississippi, Ohio, and Missouri rivers in the early-to-mid 1990s, reclaimed some forested oxbows and channels. About 27,700 acres (11,200 ha) of forested wetland were converted to deepwater habitats. Other conversions may have resulted from beaver impoundment of an area and subsequent drowning of the trees. Seventy-five percent of that area was converted to riverine channels.

Forestry practices have a substantial influence on forested wetland areas (Dahl 1999). The availability of timber used largely for processing pulp and producing paper was the basis for forestry management practices (Kovacik and Winberry 1987). Although bottomland hardwood and other wetland tree species produce valuable timber products, they are fairly slow to regenerate and mature. The average rotation age of bottomland-cypress forests in the southern United States is about 65 years (Langdon *et al.* 1981). Conversely, pines replanted in the same areas and intensively managed can attain a much shorter rotation cycle. Conversion from bottomland forest to managed pine plantations accounts for most of the changes in the freshwater forested category in the southeastern United States.

Figure 29. An example of forested wetland loss in Virginia, 1998. Trees have been cleared and the area filled for bridge construction.

A short harvest rotation can best be achieved by establishing loblolly pine (*Pinus taeda*) plantations combined with silvicultural management actions (Allen and Campbell 1988). Partial drainage combined with "bedding" has been practiced to initiate seedling regeneration in wetlands (Figure 30). By the mid 1980s, "bedding" was viewed as essential for the survival and rapid early growth of pine seedlings on poorly drained soils (Allen and Campbell 1988). The process of partial drainage and "bedding" on hydric soils results in sufficient alteration of hydrologic conditions to convert some sites to upland. Other sites planted to pine plantations remain as wetland.

Until the mid 1990s, normal silvicultural activities, including earthmoving, planting, seeding, cultivating, minor drainage and harvesting, were exempt from regulation under Section 404 of the Clean Water Act (Welsch *et al.* 1995). In 1995, the Environmental Protection Agency and the Army Corps of Engineers issued guidance at the Federal level describing "Best Management Practices" to protect water quality and hydrologic function when establishing pine plantations in wetlands. This guidance clarified the circumstances under which certain silvicultural activities were allowed in forested wetlands and outlined which mechanical silvicultural site preparation activities require a permit under the Clean Water Act (U.S. Environmental Protection Agency and Department of the Army 1995).

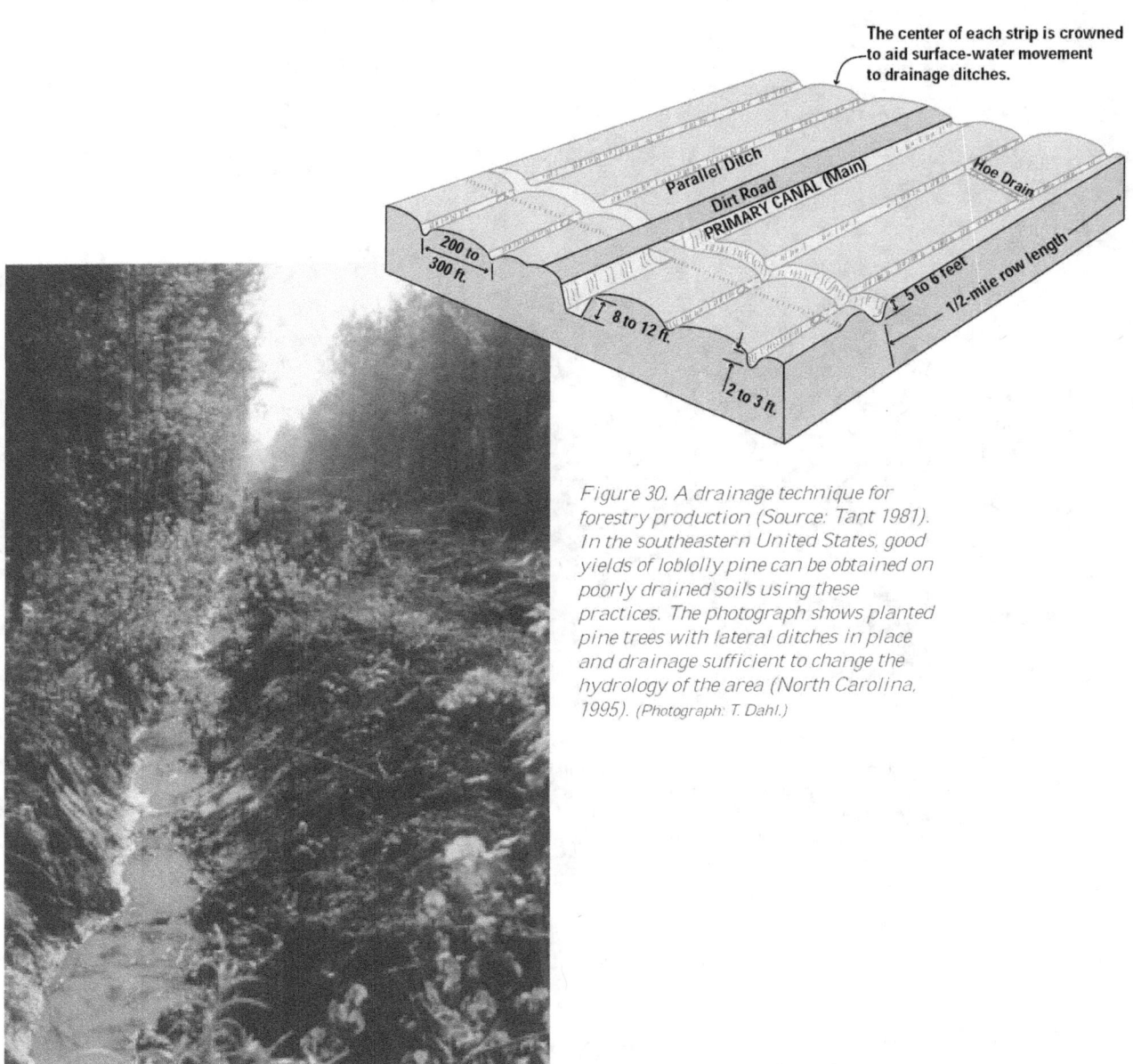

Figure 30. A drainage technique for forestry production (Source: Tant 1981). In the southeastern United States, good yields of loblolly pine can be obtained on poorly drained soils using these practices. The photograph shows planted pine trees with lateral ditches in place and drainage sufficient to change the hydrology of the area (North Carolina, 1995). (Photograph: T. Dahl.)

Documenting Changes in Land Cover

With the exception of natural disasters, change in the coastal zone often occurs one land parcel at a time. Although each action is important, the need to evaluate broad-scale change is needed.

Satellite images combined with site visits and aerial photography are the best means available to document and characterize the ground cover found over large expanses of land and near shore areas. Comparing maps made with these data from one year to the next gives an accurate picture of how communities and the coastal zone change over time.

The National Oceanic and Atmospheric Administration (NOAA), working with Federal, State, and local partners, is creating a national inventory of this information. To see examples of the imagery and a list of ongoing and completed projects, see the Web site at www.csc.noaaa.gov.

Cape Fear, North Carolina, drainage basin. *This is an unprocessed Landsat Thematic Mapper satellite image from October 31, 1996. The components of the image are analyzed, categorized, and field checked. The resulting map is an accurate documentation of the land cover that existed on that date. Comparing maps from different years provides a powerful visual and numeric representation of the changes that have occurred. (National Oceanic and Atmospheric Administration).*

Evergreen forest to grassland

Evergreen forest to scrub/shrub

Evergreen forest to bare land

Sample land cover change map for the Cape Fear drainage basin. *This image was created using satellite data from October 1991 and October 1996 and represents an area approximately nine by seven miles. Gray shades indicate areas of no land cover change. Changes due to clear cutting forestry practices are highlighted in the colored areas. Processed satellite imagery such as this was used to document land cover changes as a result of hurricanes Bertha and Fran, both of which hit this area in 1996. (National Oceanic and Atmospheric Administration.)*

Major land cover changes for the entire Cape Fear drainage basin from 1991 to 1996. From the maps and the resulting tables, State and local officials can quickly grasp how an area is changing. This sample table includes information about how many acres have been converted to development and how many acres of forest land have been lost.

Habitat Type	1991	1996	Change	Percent Change
Developed—Low Intensity	44,940	49,775	4,835	10.8
Evergreen Forest	592,644	503,565	−89,079	−15.0
Freshwater Forest	517,528	498,803	−18,725	−3.6

Freshwater Shrub Wetlands

In 1997, there were an estimated 18.4 million acres (7.5 million ha) of freshwater wetlands dominated by shrub species or wetland tree species less than 20 feet tall (6 m). The mean size of shrub wetlands sampled was 8 acres (3.2 ha). Shrub wetlands were the only vegetated freshwater wetland type to exhibit an increase in area between 1986 and 1997.

Wetland shrub trends are governed primarily by changes from freshwater forested and freshwater emergent wetlands. During this study, 2.4 million acres (970,000 ha) of shrub wetlands changed to forested wetlands, and 2.8 million acres (1.1 million ha) changed from forested wetlands to shrub wetlands. Another 1.1 million acres (445,000 ha) changed between shrub and freshwater emergent wetlands. These interactions overshadowed a 196,500 acre (79,600 ha) loss to uplands and yielded a net gain of more than 6 percent in shrub wetlands. It could not be determined if the increase in shrub wetland from emergent marsh was the result of partial drainage of emergents or due to other factors. Overall, 22 percent of shrub wetlands underwent either human induced or natural cover type changes. Losses of shrub wetlands to uplands were evenly distributed among urban and rural developments, silvicultural activities, and agriculture.

This freshwater spring supports a shrub wetland in southern Wisconsin.
(E. Ciganovich)

Freshwater shrub wetland in northern Wisconsin.

Freshwater Emergent Wetlands

Freshwater emergent wetlands occur naturally in the heart of the Nation's busiest metropolitan areas or in remote wilderness areas. This wetland type was the most easily destroyed. The mean size of freshwater emergent marshes sampled was small (7.2 acres or 2.9 ha) and they can be eliminated by surface ditching, subsurface tile drains, filling, diverting water inflows, or otherwise disrupting the confining layer in the soil (Figure 31).

Freshwater emergent wetlands sustained substantial losses from 1986 to 1997, declining by more than 1.2 million acres (496,400 ha) (4.7 percent). More than 700,000 acres (283,000 ha) of emergent wetlands were lost to upland land uses. An estimated 51 percent of emergent wetlands lost were on lands used for agriculture. Another 22 percent were lost due to development in urban or rural settings, 25 percent to areas manipulated by man but where land use was undetermined (Figure 32), and 2 percent were lost on lands converted to silviculture (Figure 33).

Freshwater emergent wetland gains included about 190,000 acres (76,900 ha) that were reclassified from freshwater forested to emergent wetlands. Another 24,000 acres (9,700 ha) were gained from changes that occurred in the deepwater category.

About 36 percent of all freshwater emergent wetlands sampled were in or adjacent to agricultural lands (Figure 34).

A.

B.

Figure 31 A–C. Examples of freshwater emergent wetland losses: (A) an emergent marsh is being filled for construction of a farm service road, South Dakota, 1999; (B) concrete and other fill materials are being added to this emergent wetland in Nebraska, 1999; (C) shallow surface ditches or drainage tiles have eliminated wetlands from this agricultural field in western Minnesota, 1999. (C: U.S. Fish and Wildlife Service)

C.

Figure 32. A freshwater emergent wetland in Tennessee (2000) that was being drained and filled. The final land use is undetermined.

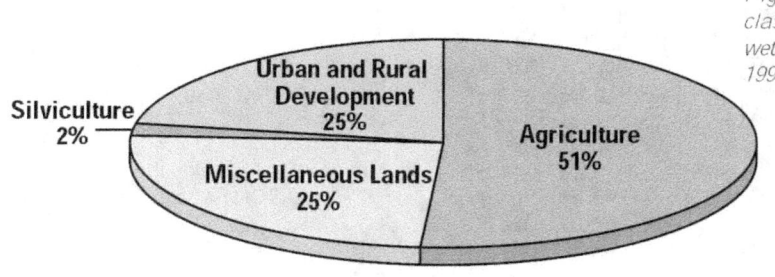

Figure 33. Current upland classification of areas where emergent wetlands were lost between 1986 and 1997.

Figure 34. A freshwater emergent wetland within an agricultural field. About 36 percent of all freshwater emergent wetlands sampled were located in or next to agriculture. (U.S. Fish and Wildlife Service)

Freshwater Ponds

The area of open water ponds in 1999 equaled the area occupied by all estuarine wetlands in the conterminous United States. The open water pond category gained the most area since the 1950s (Figure 35); there were now 5.5 million acres (2.2 million ha) of open water ponds in 1997. This was more than twice the area of open water ponds reported in the mid-1950s (Frayer *et al.* 1983). Similar trends have been reported by Moulton *et al.* (1997) who found a doubling in freshwater pond area in coastal Texas between 1955 and 1992. Bernert *et al.* (1999) also noted that freshwater ponds made the largest single contribution to wetland gains in the Willamette Valley of Oregon between 1982 and 1994.

This study included freshwater ponds that are functionally and qualitatively different. Ponds included beaver ponds, farm ponds, water retention ponds, barrow pits, small open mine pits, dug outs, small residential area lakes, water traps on golf courses, fish farms and natural ponds (Figure 36). All of these meet the wetland definition criteria of Cowardin *et al.* (1979).

An estimated 11 percent, by area, of all freshwater ponds sampled were located in or adjacent to urban areas. Many of these were created for runoff and water retention. Some were recreational or aesthetic, and others occured naturally in urban settings. The proliferation of golf courses in urban and areas of rural development has contributed substantially to the number of small freshwater ponds (Figure 37).

Forty-four percent of all ponds (by area) sampled are in or adjacent to agriculture. Many are used directly for agricultural purposes such as livestock watering, waste retention, or as recreational farm ponds (Figure 38).

The creation of larger ponds (i.e., greater than 5 acres or 2 ha), was indicative of either aquacultural development (e.g., fish farms) or surface mining operations in certain regions of the country. The increase in the number of commercial fish farms was evident in the lower Mississippi Valley States of Mississippi, Louisiana, and Arkansas (Figure 39). Nationally, the lower Mississippi Valley and central Florida contribute substantially to the number of new larger ponds created from 1986 to 1997 (Figure 40). These ponds are not an equivalent replacement for vegetated wetlands.

Some freshwater ponds have also been constructed as part of mitigation, restoration, and wetland creation efforts.

Beaver populations have further contributed to the increased number of freshwater ponds throughout many regions of the country. Several studies have discussed the importance of beaver populations and pond building to increased surface area of water (Brown *et al.* 1996; McCall *et al.* 1996).

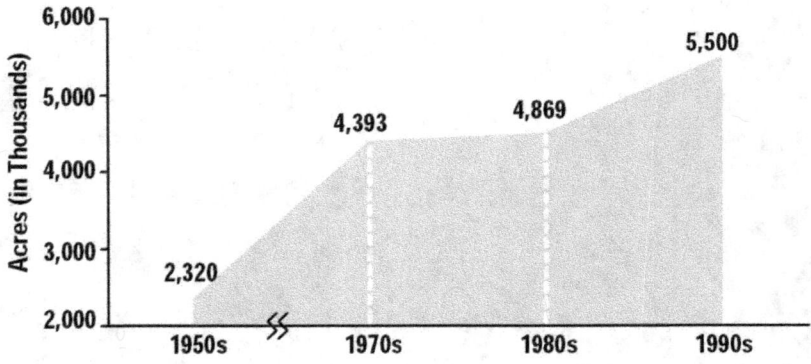

Figure 35. Long-term trends in open water ponds, 1950s to 1997. (Source: Frayer et al. 1983; Dahl and Johnson 1991; this study.)

Figure 36. Freshewater pond types vary dramatically throughout the United States. Data from this study indicate that freshwater ponds (unconsolidated bottom wetlands) have increased.
(Middle photograph: G. Latzke)

Figure 37. Contrasting color infrared aerial photographs taken in 1988 and 1999 show new ponds (dark blue or black) created as part of a golf course and housing developments (Skidaway Island, South Carolina). (National Aerial Photography Program.)

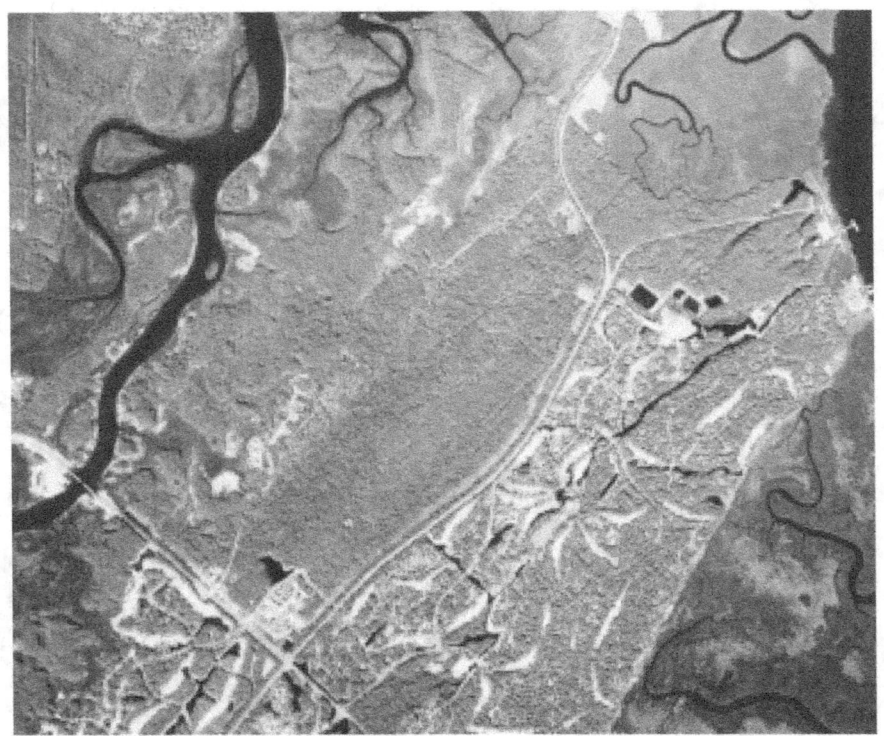

1988

1999

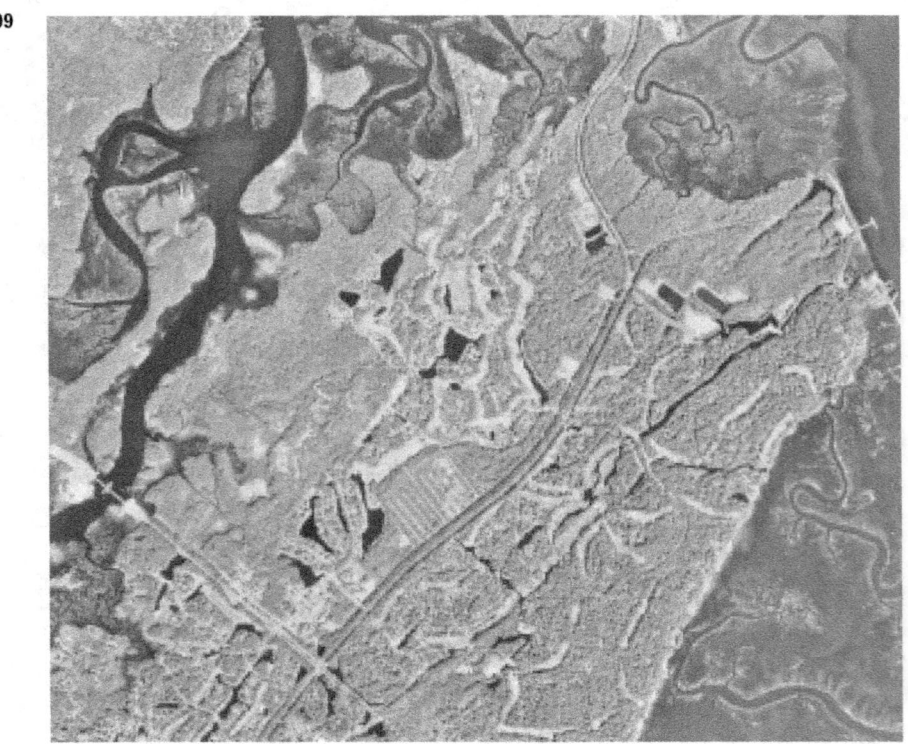

Figure 38. An excavated farm pond in northwestern Iowa, 1999.

Figure 39. Catfish farms (ponds) are shown as various shades of blue rectangles on this infrared aerial photograph from Mississippi, 1997. Aquacultural development such as this contributed to gains in the freshwater pond category. (National Aerial Photography Program)

- Small Increase in Large Ponds
- Moderate Increase in Large Ponds
- Large Increase in Large Ponds

Figure 40. Distribution and relative size of freshwater ponds created between 1986 and 1997. Concentrations of large ponds in Mississippi, Louisiana, and Arkansas are fish farms. Concentrations of larger ponds in Florida are the result of surface mining operations or construction of water retention ponds.

A playa wetland, east of Santa Fe, New Mexico.

Other Freshwater Wetlands

Freshwater unconsolidated shores were small, non-vegetated wetlands of about 3.5 acres 1.4 ha), that made up less than 0.5 percent of all freshwater wetlands. Between 1986 and 1997, freshwater unconsolidated shores exhibited an 8 percent gain in acreage or about 32,000 acres (13,000 ha). In part, this was due to peat mining operations that removed the wetland vegetation and exposed the substrate. Because these areas were not drained, they remained wetland, but their classification was changed from freshwater shrub bogs to freshwater unconsolidated shores (Figure 41). Considered anomalies, these changes were generally restricted to northern Minnesota and Maine.

Figure 41. A black-and-white aerial photograph of peat extraction (mining) in Maine, 1996. The areas indicated by a blue dot in the center have had the surface vegetation removed, but they remain wetland. The accompanying color photograph shows the peat surface. (Aerial photograph: National Aerial Photography Program)

61

Long-Term Trends in Vegetated Freshwater Wetland Types

Long-term trends of several freshwater classes are shown in Figures 42A–C. Since the 1950s, freshwater emergent wetlands have declined by the greatest percentage of any freshwater wetland type; nearly 24 percent have been lost (8 million acres or 3.2 million ha). Freshwater forested wetlands have sustained the greatest overall loss in area, declining by 10.4 million acres (4.2 million ha) since the 1950s. Both freshwater forested and emergent wetlands declined at a slower rate since the mid 1980s.

A beaver dam has impounded a stream and created this pond in Minnesota.

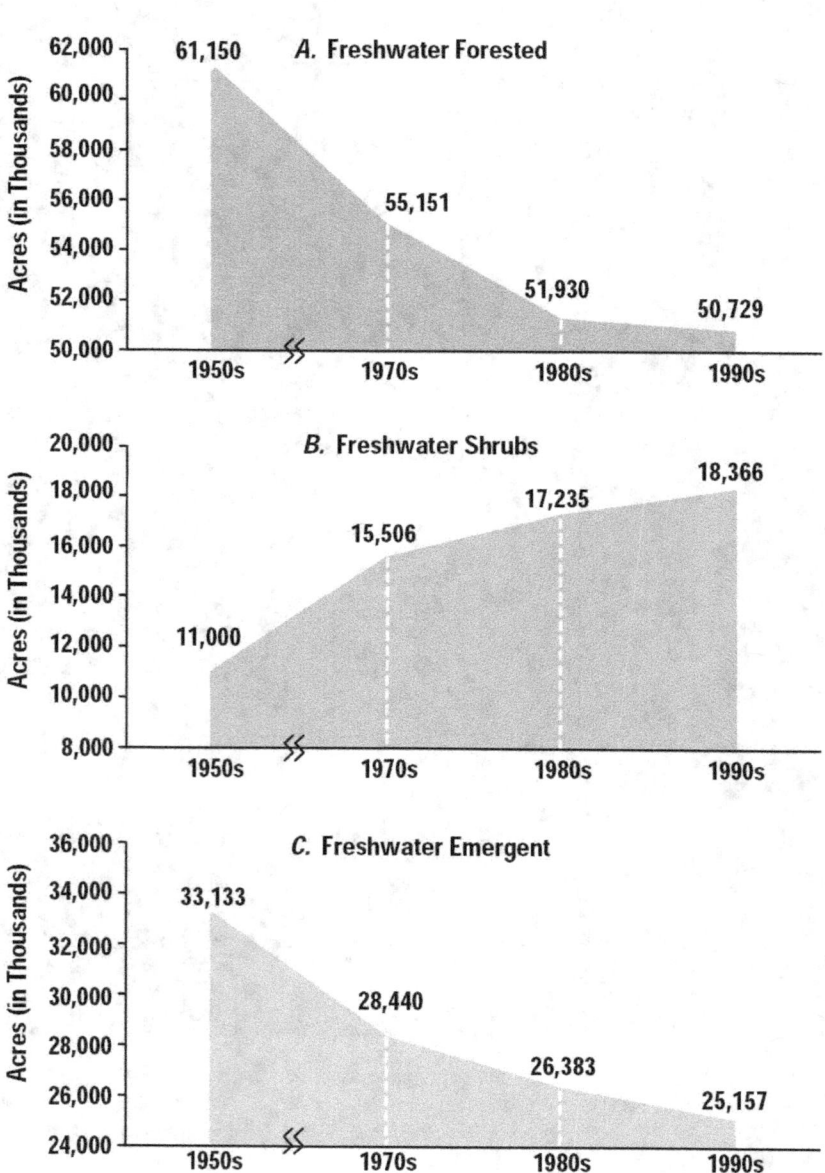

Figure 42 A–C. Long-term trends in selected freshwater wetlands, 1950s to 1997; (A) Freshwater forested wetlands; (B) freshwater shrub wetlands; (C) freshwater emergent wetlands. (Source: Frayer et al. 1983; Dahl and Johnson 1991; this study.)

Wetland Restoration, Creation and Enhancement

In the last several decades there has been considerable emphasis on wetland restoration or rehabilitation activities. Many worthwhile projects (Figure 43) have been completed by Federal, State, local, and private organizations and citizens. Various agencies and scientists have used in consistent terminology to describe ecological processes and their results. For example, "restoration" has often been used to describe the return of land area to a former condition, function, or even the enhancement of condition. Some projects designed to restore hydrologic function to degraded wetlands have not contributed area gains to the wetland base (Figure 44). Direct comparisons of wetland restoration estimates from this study with other studies using different definitions cannot be made.

Figure 43. A created wetland near Orlando, Florida, 1994.

A.

B.

Figure 44. Two oblique photographs showing A) partially drained wetlands prior to restorative actions, and B) wetland basins with restored hydrology. This example illustrates how wetland restoration has taken place with very little gain in wetland area. (U. S. Fish & Wildlife Service)

Between 1987 and 1990, programs to restore wetlands under the 1985 Food Security Act added about 90,000 acres (36,400 ha) to the Nation's wetland base (Dahl and Johnson 1991). Since that time, additional programs and initiatives such as the Conservation Reserve Program and various conservation partnership programs have been enacted to create or restore wetland acreage. This study indicated that, between 1986 and 1997, there was a net gain of wetland from "other" uplands of about 180,000 acres (72,900 ha).

Because freshwater emergent wetlands can reestablish quickly under wet conditions, there is substantial opportunity for restoration. However, from 1986 to 1997 there was a deficit between freshwater wetland losses and gains of about 630,000 acres (255,100 ha). This was due to freshwater wetland

Figure 45. Prairie wetlands in the fall of 1999 (South Dakota) have reclaimed some upland area, including the road. This form of natural restoration contributed acreage to help offset losses.

losses to urban and rural development, agriculture and silviculture.

More natural forms of restoration have also contributed to an increase in wetland area. For the first time since the 1950s, wetland area from deepwater habitats increased, mostly from riverine corridors. This suggests that the flood events of the 1990s may have reclaimed or created some wetland areas. There was also evidence that changing long-term hydrologic cycles might be contributing to the expansion of some wetland areas and creating or restoring others (Figure 45). These changes involving periods of drought followed by above average precipitation are often geographically specific and cyclical (Figure 46).

Figure 46 A and B. Color infrared aerial photographs of north-central Florida (A) 1989, during drought conditions and (B) 1996, during different hydrologic conditions. (National Aerial Photography Program)

A.

B.

Differences Between the Fish and Wildlife Service's Status and Trends and the National Resources Inventory

The Emergency Wetlands Resources Act of 1986 requires the Service to report to Congress, at ten-year intervals, on the status and trends of the Nation's wetlands. Similarly, the Natural Resources Conservation Service (NRCS) is required by legislation (Rural Development Act of 1972, Soil and Water Resources Conservation Act of 1977, and the Food Security Act of 1985 and 1990) to report at intervals of five years or less on the status of soil, water and related resources. The NRCS reports are derived from the analysis of data gathered by the National Resources Inventory (NRI). Data on resource change in both studies are gathered from the interpretation of aerial imagery supplemented with ancillary materials.

There are technical differences between the Service and the NRCS regarding how wetland data are collected, analyzed and reported (see Appendix B). For example, the Service's wetland status and trends study was designed specifically to sample wetlands and wetland change, whereas the NRI is a landscape characterization of all natural resources of which wetlands make up one component. The Service designed its study to develop wetlands trend information for all lands in the conterminous United States, whereas the NRI collects data only on non-Federal rural lands. Definitions, sampling regimes, data handling and analysis routines were developed independently as the two agencies implemented their programs over the past two decades. Each program has evolved with the assistance of spatial sampling experts and resource specialists. Because of these differences, wetland data collected by the Service and NRCS are neither comparable nor interchangeable.

A goal of the Clean Water Action Plan was to "finalize a plan to use existing inventory and data collection systems to support a single status and trends report by the Year 2000." After extensive efforts, the Department of the Interior and the Department of Agriculture concluded that it was infeasible to combine the Service's national wetlands status and trends data with NRCS data from the NRI for wetlands on non-Federal rural lands, and produce statistically reliable data for a single report on wetlands gains and losses.

Agency Differences in Estimating Wetland Loss

A major difference between the Service's wetland status and trends study and the NRCS's NRI is illustrated by the following example. A 10 acre (4 ha) parcel of a 160 acre (64.8 ha) dairy farm is made up of 8 acres (3.2 ha) of corn and 2 acres (0.8 ha) of palustrine emergent wetland. The 10 acre parcel has four wetlands each 0.5 acres (0.2 ha) in area. This parcel is sold to an individual who constructs a house, barn and other outbuildings. The landowner leaves some of the land in crop production to feed horses. In constructing the buildings, the landowner fills in 0.5 acre of wetland to build the house, 0.5 acre of wetland to build the barn, and 0.5 acre of wetland to expand a field for pasture for the horses. In this situation, the Service would record the three observed wetland losses as: **house construction =** *loss to rural development;* **barn construction =** *loss to agriculture;* **pasture expansion =** *loss to agriculture.*

The instructions for the 1997 National Resources Inventory (Point Module III, Land Use, P. 11) indicate that this would be an example of a "rural estate" under the "Residential" category. Rural estates are defined as,

"A land use category (under residential) that includes rural residences that are not part of an operating farm and have no intensive agricultural enterprises. They may include small pastures for livestock grazing and may have structures such as garages or barns, with no special use buildings such as poultry or hog houses or mink ranches."

Rural estates generally have a 10 acre size limit. In this example, the NRI would record this as a 10 acre loss to rural development.

A freshwater wetland in Louisiana.
(U.S. Fish and Wildlife Service)

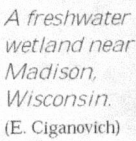

A freshwater wetland near Madison, Wisconsin.
(E. Ciganovich)

Summary

This study estimated wetland status and trends using 4,375 four square mile sample plots. Twenty one percent of the plots were field verified and rigorous quality control measures were taken to ensure data integrity and quality. The findings indicate that an estimated 105.5 million acres (42.7 million ha) of wetlands remained in the conterminous United States. The average annual net loss of wetlands was 58,500 acres (23,700 ha), a decline of 80 percent from the previous decade. This decline in the rate of wetland loss was attributed to Federal programs such as the conservation provisions of the Food Security Act, Conservation Reserve Program, Fish and Wildlife Service's conservation and restoration partnership programs, environmental education and other State sponsored conservation initiatives.

Estuarine wetlands made up 5 percent of the total area of wetlands found in the conterminous United States. Estuarine emergents declined by 14,450 acres (5,850 ha), a 0.4 percent loss from 1986 to 1997. Fifty eight percent of the losses were from some form of deepwater intrusion into the wetland. Estuarine non-vegetated intertidal wetlands declined slightly (0.1 percent), but marine intertidal beaches declined 1.7 percent. Marine and estuarine wetland areas accounted for two percent of the losses.

Between 1986 and 1997, wetlands declined by an estimated 644,000 acres (260,700 ha). Ninety-eight percent of these losses were to freshwater wetland types. The loss rate of freshwater forested wetlands declined from 6.2 percent between the 1970s to the 1980s, to 2.3 percent in this study. Freshwater emergent wetlands experienced a substantial loss in area, with a net change of nearly 1.2 million acres (485,800 ha). Shrub wetlands were the only vegetated freshwater wetland type that exhibited an increase in area.

Urban development accounted for 30 percent of the wetland losses to upland; agriculture 26 percent; silviculture 23 percent, and rural development 21 percent.

Long-term trends indicate that freshwater emergent wetlands have declined by the greatest percentage of any freshwater wetland type; nearly 24 percent have been lost. Freshwater forested wetlands have sustained the greatest overall loss in area, declining by 10.4 million acres since the 1950s.

Open water ponds increased in area by about 13 percent during this study. There were 5.5 million acres (2.2 million ha) of ponds, more than twice the area of open water ponds reported in the mid 1950s. The creation of large ponds (greater than 5 acres or 2 ha), was the result of aquiculture (fish farms), surface mining operations or water retention ponds constructed in certain regions of the country. These ponds were not equivalent replacement for vegetated wetlands.

Among the wetlands sampled, 55 percent were located in or adjacent to "other" uplands. An additional 31 percent were in or adjacent to agricultural lands; 24 percent in or adjacent to upland silviculture; and 5 were in or adjacent to urban upland areas (percentages exceed 100 because some wetlands are adjacent to more than one upland category).

Deepwater lakes and reservoirs exhibited a modest increase in area with a net gain of 116,400 acres (47,100 ha). The rate of lake and reservoir creation declined 43 percent from the previous decade.

There were net gains to wetlands from both inland deepwater habitats (primarily rivers), and from "other" lands. Long-term hydrologic cycles might be contributing to the expansion of some wetland areas and creating or restoring others. The reduction in wetland losses coupled with restoration and creation of wetland area is helping the Nation approach its no net loss in wetland goal.

Wetland along the St. Louis River in northeastern Minnesota.

Literature Cited

Allen, H.L. and R.G. Campbell. 1988. Wet site pine management in the Southeastern United States. *In*: D.D. Hook, W.H. McKee, Jr., H.K. Smith, J. Gregory, V.G. Burrell, Jr., M.R. DeVoe, R.E. Sojka, S. Gilbert, R. Banks, L.H. Stolzy, C. Brooks, T.D. Matthews, and T.H. Shear (eds.). The ecology and management of wetlands. Vol. 2. Timber Press, Portland, OR. pp. 173–184.

Anderson, J.R., E.E. Hardy, J.T. Roach and R.E. Winter. 1976. A land use and land cover classification system for use with remote sensor data. U.S. Geological Survey Professional Paper 964. U.S. Geological Survey, Washington, D.C. 28 p.

Barras, J.A., P.E. Bourgeois, and L.R. Handley. 1994. Land loss in coastal Louisiana 1956–90. National Biological Survey, National Wetlands Research Center Open File Report 94–01. 4 p. + color plates.

Bernert, J.A., J.A., J.M. Eilers. B.J. Eilers, E. Blok. S.G. Daggett and E.F. Bierly. 1999. Recent wetlands trends (1981/82–1994) in the Willamette Valley, Oregon, USA. Wetlands, Vol. 19, No. 3. pp. 545–559.

Britsch, L.D. and J.B. Dunbar. 1993. Land loss rates: Louisiana coastal plain. Journal of Coastal Research, 9. pp. 324–338.

Brown, D.J., W.A Hubert, and S.H. Anderson. 1996. Beaver ponds create wetland habitat for birds in mountains of southeastern Wyoming. Wetlands. Vol. 16, No. 2. pp. 127–133.

Charbreck, R.H. 1988. Coastal Marshes—Ecology and wildlife management. Univ. of Minnesota Press, Minneapolis, MN. 138 p.

Cowardin, L.M, V. Carter, F.C. Golet, and E.T. LaRoe. 1979. Classification of wetlands and deepwater habitats of the United States. Department of the Interior. U.S. Fish and Wildlife Service, Washington, D.C. 131 p.

Culliton, T.J. 1998. Pressures on coastal environments—Population: distribution, density and growth. NOAA's State of the Coast Report. National Oceanic and Atmospheric Administration, Silver Spring, MD.

Dahl, T.E. 1999. South Carolina's wetlands—status and trends 1982–1989. Department of the Interior, U.S. Fish and Wildlife Service, Washington, D.C. 58 p.

Dahl, T.E. 1990. Wetlands losses in the United States 1780s to 1980s. Department of the Interior, U.S. Fish and Wildlife Service, Washington, D.C. 21 p.

Dahl, T.E. and C.E. Johnson. 1991. Status and trends of wetlands in the conterminous United States, mid-1970s to mid-1980s. U.S. Department of the Interior. U.S. Fish and Wildlife Service, Washington, D.C. 28 p.

Ferguson, R.L., L.L. Wood and D.B. Graham. 1993. Monitoring spatial change in seagrass habitat with aerial photography. Photogrammetric Engineering and Remote Sensing, 59(6). pp. 1033–1038.

Field, D.W., A.J. Reyer, P.V. Genovese and B.D. Shearer. 1991. Coastal wetlands of the United States—An accounting of a valuable national resource. Strategic Assessment Branch, Ocean Assessments Division, Office of Oceanography and Marine Assessment, National Ocean Service, Nation Oceanic and Atmospheric Administration, Rockville, MD. 59 p.

Florida Department of Environmental Protection. 1994. An assessment of invasive non-indigenous species in Florida's public lands. Department of Environmental Protection, Tallahassee, FL.

Fonseca, M.S., Kenworthy, W.J. and G.W. Thayer. 1998. Guidelines for the conservation and restoration of seagrasses in the United States and adjacent waters. NOAA Coastal Ocean Program Decision Analysis Series No. 12, NOAA

Coastal Ocean Office, Silver Spring, MD. 222 p.

Frankenburg, D. 1995. The nature of the Outer Banks. Environmental processes, field sites, and developmental issues, Corolla to Ocracoke. Univ. of North Carolina Press, Chapel Hill, NC. 142 pp.

Frayer, W.E., T.J. Monahan, D.C. Bowden, and F.A. Graybill. 1983. Status and trends of wetlands and deepwater habitats in the conterminous United States, 1950's to 1970's. Colorado State University, Fort Collins, CO. 31 p.

Good, J.W., J.W. Weber, J.W. Charland, J.V. Olson and K.A. Chapin. 1997. State coastal zone management effectiveness in protecting estuaries and coastal wetlands: A national overview. Oregon Sea Grant, Oregon State Univ., Corvallis, OR. 283 p.

Hammond, E.H. 1970. Physical subdivisions of the United States of America. *In:* U.S. Geological Survey. National atlas of the United States of America. Department of the Interior, Washington, D.C. 61 p.

Hefner, J.M., B.O. Wilen, T.E. Dahl and W.E. Frayer. 1994. Southeast wetlands; status and trends, mid-1970's to mid-1980's. Department of the Interior, U.S. Fish and Wildlife Service, Atlanta, GA. 32 p.

Kovacik, C.F. and J.J. Winberry. 1987. South Carolina A Geography. Westview Press, Boulder, CO. 235 p.

Langbein, W.B. and K.T. Iseri. 1960. General introduction and hydrologic definitions manual of hydrology. Part 1. General surface water techniques. U.S. Geological Survey, Water Supply Paper 1541–A. 29 p.

Langdon, O.G., J.P. McClure, D.D. Hook, J.M. Crockett and R. Hunt. 1981. Extent, condition, management, and research needs of bottomland hardwood—cypress forests in the Southeastern United States. *In:* J.R. Clark and J. Benforado (eds.). Wetlands of bottomland hardwood forests. Elsevier Scientific Pub. Co. Amsterdam, The Netherlands. pp. 71–85.

Lanyon J.M., C.J. Limpus and H. Marsh. 1989. Dugongs and turtles: grazers in the seagrass system. *In:* A.W.D. Larkum, A.J. McComb and S.A. Sheperd (eds.). Biology of Seagrasses. Elsevier Science Pub. Amsterdam, The Netherlands. pp. 610–634.

McCall, T.C., T.P. Hodgman, D.R. Diefenbach and R.B Owen, Jr. 1996. Beaver populations and their relation to wetland habitat and breeding waterfowl in Maine. Wetlands. Vol. 16, No.2. pp.163–172.

McCann, J.A., L.N. Arkin and J.D. Williams. 1996. Nonindigenous aquatic and selected terrestrial species of Florida. Univ. of Florida, Center for Aquatic Plants, Gainesville, FL.

Moulton, D.W., T.E. Dahl and D.M. Dall. 1997. Texas coastal wetlands—status and trends, mid-1950s to early 1990s. United States Department of the Interior, U.S. Fish and Wildlife Service, Albuquerque, NM. 32 p.

Reed, P.B. 1988. National list of plant species that occur in wetlands: NERC–88/18.40. Department of the Interior. U.S. Fish and Wildlife Service, Washington, D.C.

Sallenger, A.H. and S.J. Williams. 1989. U.S. Geological Survey studies of Louisiana barrier island erosion and wetland loss. Open-File Report 89–372. Department of the Interior, U.S. Geological Survey, Reston, VA. 17 p.

Sarndal, C-E., B. Swensson and J. Wretman. 1992. Model assisted survey sampling. Springer-Verlag, New York, NY.

Shapiro, C. 1995. Coordination and integration of wetland data for status and trends and inventory estimates. Technical Report 2. Federal Geographic Data Committee, Wetlands Subcommittee, Washington, D.C. 210 p.

Tansey, J.B. and N.D. Cost. 1990. Estimating the forest-wetland resource in the southeastern United States with forest survey data. *In:* B.D. Jackson(ed). Forest Ecology and Management Vol. 33/34, Nos. 1–4. pp. 193–213.

Tant, P.L. 1981. Soil survey of Washington County, North Carolina. USDA, Soil Conservation Service in cooperation with NC Ag. Res. Service, NC Ag. Extension Service, Washington Co. Board of Commissioners and NC Dept. of Nat. Res. and Community Development. 99 p.

Thayer, G.W., W.J. Kenworthy and M..S. Fonseca. 1984. The ecology of eelgrass meadows of the Atlantic coast: a community profile. Department of the Interior. U.S.

Fish and Wildlife Service. FWS/OBS—84/02. 147 p. Reprinted September, 1985.

The Conservation Foundation . 1988. Protecting America's wetlands: an action agenda. Final Report of the National Wetlands Policy Forum. Washington, D.C. 69 p.

Thompson, S.K. 1992. Sampling. John Wiley and Sons, Inc., New York, NY.

Tiner, R.W. Jr. 1984. Wetlands of the United States: Current status and recent trends. Department of the Interior. U.S. Fish and Wildlife Service. Washington, D.C. 59 p.

U.S. Department of Agriculture. 1975. Soil taxonomy: A basic system of soil classification for making and interpreting soil surveys. U.S. Department of Agriculture. Soil Conservation Service, Soil Survey Staff, Agricultural Handbook 436, Washington, D.C. 754 p.

U.S. Department of Agriculture. 1991. Hydric Soils of the United States. Soil Conservation Service, Miscellaneous Publication Number 1491, Washington, D.C.

U.S. Environmental Protection Agency. 1979. Handbook for analytical quality control in water and wastewater laboratories. EPA–6–/4–79–019. Office of Research and Development, Cincinnati, OH.

U.S. Environmental Protection Agency and U.S. Department of the Army. 1995. Memorandum to the field—Application of best management practices to mechanical silvicultural site preparation activities for the establishment of pine plantations in the southeast. Washington, D.C. 8 p.

U.S. Fish and Wildlife Service. 1994a. Continuous wetlands trend analysis project specifications (photo-interpretation and cartographic procedures). Wetland Status and Trends, National Wetlands Inventory Center, St. Petersburg, FL. 60 p.

U.S. Fish and Wildlife Service. 1994b. Technical specifications and protocols for Status and Trends digital files. Wetland Status and Trends, National Wetlands Inventory Center, St. Petersburg, FL. 35 p. plus appendices.

U.S. Fish and Wildlife Service. 1995. Coastal Ecosystems Program. Branch of Coastal and Wetland Resources, Division of Habitat Conservation, Washington, D.C. 48 p.

Welsch, D.J., D.L. Smart, J.N. Boyer, P. Minkin, H.C. Smith and T. L. McCandless. 1995. Forested wetlands: Functions, benefits and the use of best management practices. U.S. Department of Agriculture, Forest Service. NA–PR–01–95, Radnor, PA. 63 p.

White, W.A. and T.A. Tremblay. 1994. Submergence of wetlands as a result of human-induced subsidence and faulting along the upper Texas Gulf coast. Bureau of Economic Geology, The University of Texas at Austin, Austin, TX. 42 p.

Whitlatch, R.B. 1982. The ecology of New England tidal flats: a community profile. U.S. Fish and Wildlife Service, Washington. D.C. FWS/OBS-81/01. 125 p.

Zieman, J.C. 1982. The ecology of the seagrasses of south Florida: a community profile. U.S. Fish and Wildlife Service, Washington, D.C. FWS/OBS–82/25. 158 p

A forested wetland in Oregon.

Appendix A.

Definitions of Habitat Categories Used in this Status and Trends Study

Wetlands[1]

In general terms, wetlands are lands where saturation with water is the dominant factor determining the nature of soil development and the types of plant and animal communities living in the soil and on its surface. The single feature that most wetlands share is soil or substrate that is at least periodically saturated with or covered by water. The water creates severe physiological problems for all plants and animals except those that are adapted for life in water or in saturated soil.

Wetlands are lands transitional between terrestrial and aquatic systems where the water table is usually at or near the surface or the land is covered by shallow water. For purposes of this classification wetlands must have one or more of the following three attributes: (1) at least periodically, the land supports predominantly hydrophytes,[2] (2) the substrate is predominantly undrained hydric soil, [3] and (3) the substrate is non-soil and is saturated with water or covered by shallow water at some time during the growing season of each year.

The term wetland includes a variety of areas that fall into one of five categories: (1) areas with hydrophytes and hydric soils, such as those commonly known as marshes, swamps, and bogs; (2) areas without hydrophytes but with hydric soils—for example, flats where drastic fluctuation in water level, wave action, turbidity, or high concentration of salts may prevent the growth of hydrophytes; (3) areas with hydrophytes but non-hydric soils, such as margins of impoundments or excavations where hydrophytes have become established but hydric soils have not yet developed; (4) areas without soils but with hydrophytes such as the seaweed-covered portions of rocky shores; and (5) wetlands without soil and without hydrophytes, such as gravel beaches or rocky shores without vegetation.

Marine System

The marine system consists of the open ocean overlying the continental shelf and its associated high energy coastline. Marine habitats are exposed to the waves and currents of the open ocean. Salinities exceed 30 parts per thousand, with little or no dilution except outside the mouths of estuaries. Shallow coastal indentations or bays without appreciable freshwater inflow and coasts with exposed rocky islands that provide the mainland with little or no shelter from wind and waves, are also considered part of the marine system because they generally support typical marine biota.

Estuarine System

The estuarine system consists of deepwater tidal habitats and adjacent tidal wetland that are usually semi-enclosed by land but have open, partly obstructed, or sporadic access to the open ocean, and in which ocean water is at least occasionally diluted by freshwater runoff from the land. The salinity may be periodically increased above that of the open ocean by evaporation. Along some low energy coastlines there is appreciable dilution of sea water. Offshore areas with typical estuarine plants and animals, such as red mangroves (*Rhizophora mangle*) and eastern oysters (*Crassostrea virginica*), are also included in the estuarine system.

Beach re-establishment in Florida.

---

[1]Adapted from Cowardin *et al.* 1979.

[2]The U.S. Fish and Wildlife Service has published the list of plant species that occur in wetlands of the United States (Reed 1988).

[3]U.S. Department of Agriculture has developed the list of hydric soils for the United States (U.S. Department of Agriculture 1991).

Marine and Estuarine Subsystems

Subtidal The substrate is continuously submerged by marine or estuarine waters.

Intertidal The substrate is exposed and flooded by tides. Intertidal includes the splash zone of coastal waters.

Palustrine System

The palustrine (freshwater) system includes all non-tidal wetlands dominated by trees, shrubs, persistent emergents, emergent mosses or lichens, farmed wetlands, and all such wetlands that occur in tidal areas where salinity due to ocean derived salts is below 0.5 parts per thousand. It also includes wetlands lacking such vegetation, but with all of the following four characteristics: (1) area less than 20 acres (8 ha); (2) active wave formed or bedrock shoreline features are lacking; (3) water depth in the deepest part of basin less than 6.6 feet (2 meters) at low water; and (4) salinity due to ocean derived salts less than 0.5 parts per thousand.

Classes

Unconsolidated Bottom Unconsolidated bottom includes all wetlands with at least 25 percent cover of particles smaller than stones, and a vegetative cover less than 30 percent. Examples of unconsolidated substrates are: sand, mud, organic material, cobble-gravel.

Aquatic Bed Aquatic beds are dominated by plants that grow principally on or below the surface of the water for most of the growing season in most years. Examples include seagrass beds[4], pondweeds (*Potamogeton spp.*), wild celery (*Vallisneria americana*), waterweed (*Elodea spp.*), and duckweed (*Lemna spp.*).

Rocky Shore Rocky shore includes wetland environments characterized by bedrock, stones, or boulders which singly or in combination have an areal cover of 75 percent or more and an areal vegetative coverage of less than 30 percent.

Unconsolidated Shore Unconsolidated shore includes all wetland habitats having two characteristics: (1) unconsolidated substrates with less than 75 percent areal cover of stones, boulders or bedrock and; (2) less than 30 percent areal cover of vegetation other than pioneering plants.

Emergent Wetland Emergent wetlands are characterized by erect, rooted, herbaceous hydrophytes, excluding mosses and lichens. This vegetation is present for most of the growing season in most years. These wetlands are usually dominated by perennial plants.

Shrub Wetland Shrub wetlands include areas dominated by woody vegetation less than 20 feet (6 meters) tall. The species include true shrubs, young trees, and trees or shrubs that are small or stunted because of environmental conditions.

Forested Wetland Forested wetlands are characterized by woody vegetation that is 20 feet (6 meters) tall or taller.

Palustrine Farmed Farmed wetlands are wetlands that meet the Cowardin *et al.* definition where the soil surface has been mechanically or physically altered for production of crops, but where hydrophytes will become re-established if farming is discontinued.

A forested wetland in a river bottom in Tennessee.

---

[4]Although some seagrass beds may be evident on aerial photography, water and climatic conditions often prevent their detection.

Deepwater Habitats

Wetlands and deepwater habitats are defined separately because the term wetland has not included deep permanent water bodies. For the purposes of conducting status and trends studies, riverine and lacustrine are considered deepwater habitats. Elements of marine or estuarine systems can be wetland or deepwater. Palustrine includes only wetland habitats.

Deepwater habitats are permanently flooded land lying below the deepwater boundary of wetlands. Deepwater habitats include environments where surface water is permanent and often deep, so that water, rather than air, is the principal medium within which the dominant organisms live, whether or not they are attached to the substrate. As in wetlands, the dominant plants are hydrophytes; however, the substrates are considered non-soil because the water is too deep to support emergent vegetation (U.S. Department of Agriculture 1975).

Riverine System The riverine system includes deepwater habitats contained within a channel, with the exception of habitats with water containing ocean derived salts in excess of 0.5 parts per thousand. A channel is "an open conduit either naturally or artificially created which periodically or continuously contains moving water, or which forms a connecting link between two bodies of standing water" (Langbein and Iseri 1960).

Lacustrine System The lacustrine system includes deepwater habitats with all of the following characteristics: (1) situated in a topographic depression or a dammed river channel; (2) lacking trees, shrubs, persistent emergents, emergent mosses or lichens with greater than 30 percent coverage; (3) total area exceeds 20 acres (8 ha). Similar wetland and deepwater habitats totaling less than 20 acres may also be included in the Lacustrine System if an active, wave-formed or bedrock shoreline feature makes up all or part of the boundary, or if the water depth in the deepest part of the basin exceeds 6.6 feet (2 meters) at low water.

The Green Peter Reservoir, a deepwater habitat in Oregon.

Uplands

Agriculture[5]

Agricultural land may be defined broadly as land used primarily for production of food and fiber. Agricultural activity is evidenced by distinctive geometric field and road patterns on the landscape and the traces produced by livestock or mechanized equipment. Examples of agricultural land use include cropland and pasture; orchards, groves, vineyards, nurseries, cultivated lands, and ornamental horticultural areas including sod farms; confined feeding operations; and other agricultural land including livestock feed lots, farmsteads including houses, support structures (silos) and adjacent yards, barns, poultry sheds, etc.

Urban

Urban land is comprised of areas of intensive use in which much of the land is covered by structures (high building density). Urbanized areas are cities and towns that provide the goods and services needed to survive by modern day standards through a central business district. Services such as banking, medical and legal office buildings, supermarkets, and department stores make up the business center of a city. Commercial strip developments along main transportation routes, shopping centers, contiguous dense residential areas, industrial and commercial complexes, transportation, power and communication facilities, city parks, ball fields and golf courses can also be included in the urban category.

Forested Plantation

Forested plantations include areas of planted and managed forest stands. Planted pines, Christmas tree farms, clear cuts, and other managed forest stands, such as hardwood forestry are included in this category.

Forested plantations can be identified by observing the following remote sensing indicators: 1) trees planted in rows or blocks; 2) forested blocks growing with uniform crown heights; and 3) logging activity and use patterns.

---

[5] Adapted from Anderson *et al.* 1976.

Figure 47. An example of upland "other" shrub steppe in Montana, 1999.

Rural Development

Rural developments occur in sparse rural and suburban settings outside distinct urban cities and towns. They are characterized by non-intensive land use and sparse building density. Typically, a rural development is a cross-roads community that has a corner gas station and a convenience store which are surrounded by sparse residential housing and agriculture. Scattered suburban communities located outside of a major urban center can also be included in this category as well as some industrial and commercial complexes; isolated transportation, power, and communication facilities; strip mines; quarries; and recreational areas such as golf courses, etc. Major highways through rural development areas are included in the rural development category.

Other Land Use

Other Land Use is composed of uplands not characterized by the previous categories. Typically these lands would include native prairie; unmanaged or non-patterned upland forests and scrub lands; and barren land (Figure 47). Lands in transition may also fit into this category. Transitional lands are lands in transition from one land use to another. They generally occur in large acreage blocks of 40 acres (16 ha) or more and are characterized by the lack of any remote sensor information that would enable the interpreter to reliably predict future use. The transitional phase occurs when wetlands are drained, ditched, filled, leveled, or the vegetation has been removed and the area is temporarily bare.

A freshwater wetland in Nevada.

Appendix B.
Contrasting the Fish and Wildlife Service's Status and Trends with the Natural Resource Conservation Service's National Resources Inventory[1]

	FWS—Status and Trend	NRCS—NRI
Methods[2]	· Stratified random sample of 4,375 4-square mile plots. · Includes all lands, Federal and non-Federal. · Plots are weighted by expected wetland density. · Special stratum added to include all coastal wetland resources.	· Probability based random sample of 800,00 points restricted to private lands. · Principal focus is on commodity crop production. · 60,000 to 80,000 points in aquatic habitats. · NRI does not sample all coastal wetlands.
Purpose	· Congressionally mandated by the Emergency Wetlands Resources Act to report on status and trends of wetlands. · Focus is entirely on wetlands. · Produces a specific report on status and trends outlining procedures, definitions, results and statistical validity.	· Congressionally mandated by the Rural Development Act, Soil and Water Conservation Act and Food Security Act. · Landscape characterization of natural resources of which wetlands are one component. · Specific purpose is to monitor lands in agricultural production. · Reports on the status of natural resources with wetlands being one component. · Produces press releases, informational flyers, news releases, web based summaries and articles.
Report Frequency	· Ten-year cycle	· Five-year cycle
Data Collection	· Aerial imagery used in conjunction with collateral data and field work. — Soil surveys; — Topographic quads; — NOAA navigation charts; — National Wetlands Inventory (NWI) maps. · Uses a small cadre of wetland interpreters that averaged 12 years experience in wetland identification and classification.	· Soil surveys used as the primary data source. · Topographic quads, or other base map(s). · 35mm color or black and white slides · NWI maps.. · Uses hundreds of NRCS employees of many disciplines nationwide for data collection work.
Quality Assurance	· Quality control steps included in various processes throughout the data collection, analysis steps. · Field verification of 21% of the plots. · Six Federal agencies assisted with field verification work for the year 2000 status and trends report.	· Computer generated data verification with up to 2% field verification of all points.

	FWS—Status and Trend	NRCS—NRI
Technical Differences		
• **Deepwater Lakes**	· Classifies water bodies 20 acres (8.1 ha) or greater as deepwater lakes. Water bodies less than 20 acres are classified as ponds. · Does not include any persistent emergent vegetation in the lacustrine system (lakes).	· Classifies any water body 6.6 feet (2 m) or deeper as deepwater lakes. · Includes some emergent vegetation in the lacustrine system (lakes).
• **Development**	· Classifies developed areas into 2 general categories; urban and rural.	· Classifies developed areas into small and large based on structure density.
• **Forested Wetlands**	· Uses leaf-off imagery to identify forested wetlands. Bases forested wetland extent on visible indications of hydrology in conjunction with collateral data sources. Some managed pine plantations that have been extensively drained are considered uplands.	· Uses 35 mm slides often taken during the peak of the growing season (leaf-on). Classifies forest cover occurring on hydric soils as wetland. Pine plantations on hydric soils are considered forested wetland.
• **Ephemeral Wetlands**	· Ephemeral wetlands are not part of the Cowardin *et al.* (1979) classification and thus, are not included.	· Includes wetland types characterized by ephemeral hydrology.
• **Wetland Shrubs**	· Identifies all wetlands with woody vegetation 20 feet (6 m) or less as shrub wetlands.	· Identifies tree species less than 20 feet tall as forested wetlands. Shrub species are identified as shrub wetlands.
• **Food Security Act (FSA) Wetlands**	· Does not differentiate FSA wetland types.	· Uses the Cowardin *et al.* definition as well as the FSA definition of wetlands. FSA differentiates some wetland and non wetland types to include "farmed wetlands", and "Prior converted wetlands" which are non-wetland for FSA purposes. In addition, Cowardin wetlands may be assigned a cropped covertype if in agricultural production.

[1.] *Also see Shapiro (1995) for a review of the level of consistency among data sets.*

[2.] *The Service has consulted with leading spatial sampling experts regarding the merging of different sampling schemes and the likelihood of producing a single set of wetland change figures. The consensus from inside and outside the Federal government is that statistically designed sampling approaches, developed independently, such as this study and the NRI cannot be combined to produce statistically reliable data.*

Appendix C.

This table presents estimates of acreage by classification and the number of acres that changed classification between 1986 and 1997. The rows identify the 1986 classification. The columns identify the classification and acreage of 1997. The number under the acreage estimate for each entry is the percent coefficient variation for that estimate.

1997 Classification, Estimated Acreage, and Percent Coefficient of Variation. Values shown as: acreage (percent coefficient of variation).

1986 Group	1986 Classification	Marine Subtidal	Marine Intertidal	Estuarine Subtidal	Estuarine Aquatic Bed	Estuarine Emergents	Estuarine Forested Shrub	Estuarine Unconsolidated Shore	Palustrine Aquatic Bed	Palustrine Emergents	Palustrine Forested
Saltwater Habitats	Marine Subtidal	1742501 (32)	1263 (51)	25071 (95)	0 (—)	0 (—)	0 (—)	1589 (69)	0 (—)	0 (—)	0 (—)
	Marine Intertidal	1284 (44)	127164 (20)	316 (67)	0 (—)	58 (96)	152 (78)	3192 (44)	0 (—)	0 (—)	0 (—)
	Estuarine Subtidal	33 (95)	380 (54)	17592291 (2)	453 (95)	15287 (19)	470 (43)	26027 (20)	0 (—)	51 (98)	0 (—)
	Estuarine Aquatic Bed	0 (—)	0 (—)	0 (—)	28831 (27)	0 (—)	0 (—)	228 (73)	0 (—)	0 (—)	0 (—)
	Estuarine Emergents	10 (95)	1339 (59)	23616 (15)	0 (—)	3908918 (4)	12139 (33)	3912 (25)	0 (—)	485 (43)	0 (—)
	Estuarine Forested Shrub	68 (95)	126 (65)	1278 (45)	0	5733 (55)	656001 (13)	509 (44)	0 (—)	0 (—)	0 (—)
	Estuarine Unconsolidated Shore	407 (95)	437 (59)	19157 (19)	0	10039 (18)	3891 (44)	514336 (11)	0 (—)	50 (67)	0 (—)
Freshwater Habitats	Palustrine Aquatic Bed	0 (—)	0 (—)	0 (—)	0 (—)	0 (—)	0 (—)	0 (—)	219135 (13)	18044 (31)	444 (52)
	Palustrine Emergents	0 (—)	0 (—)	7 (94)	0 (—)	0 (—)	48 (96)	0 (—)	5504 (49)	23875051 (9)	362951 (15)
	Palustrine Forested	0 (—)	0 (—)	39 (104)	0 (—)	72 (98)	0 (—)	0 (—)	5719 (36)	550747 (9)	47967327 (3)
	Palustrine Shrub	0 (—)	0 (—)	242 (58)	0 (—)	27 (97)	0 (—)	43 (95)	347 (50)	204309 (9)	2365784 (8)
	Palustrine Unconsolidated Bottom	0 (—)	0 (—)	66 (61)	0 (—)	0 (—)	0 (—)	0 (—)	3752 (30)	86403 (12)	2948 (30)
	Palustrine Unconsolidate Shore	0 (—)	0 (—)	0 (—)	0 (—)	0 (—)	0 (—)	0 (—)	0 (—)	11459 (30)	85 (76)
Cultivated Rice		0 (—)	0 (—)	0 (—)	0 (—)	0 (—)	0 (—)	0 (—)	0 (—)	12626 (33)	5737 (76)
Deepwater Habitats	Lacustrine	0 (—)	0 (—)	14 (94)	0 (—)	0 (—)	0 (—)	0 (—)	1054 (58)	118445 (18)	603 (99)
	Riverine	0 (—)	0 (—)	0 (—)	0 (—)	0 (—)	0 (—)	0 (—)	0 (—)	60230 (55)	9364 (57)
Uplands	Agricultural	0 (—)	0 (—)	131 (62)	0 (—)	285 (55)	0 (—)	0 (—)	3988 (74)	162063 (20)	2606 (46)
	Urban	0 (—)	0 (—)	214 (53)	0 (—)	0 (—)	0 (—)	221 (78)	261 (93)	868 (46)	41 (100)
	Upland Forested Plantation	0 (—)	0 (—)	204 (95)	0 (—)	24 (95)	0 (—)	0 (—)	621 (72)	6394 (44)	3054 (43)
	Upland Rural Development	0 (—)	0 (—)	222 (86)	0 (—)	0 (—)	0 (—)	41 (96)	0 (—)	3972 (39)	201 (99)
	Other	0 (—)	146 (76)	1052 (26)	0 (—)	2026 (52)	79 (69)	730 (36)	3006 (57)	45938 (35)	7353 (29)
Acreage Totals, 1997		1744303 (32)	130855 (20)	17663922 (2)	29284 (27)	3942468 (4)	672781 (13)	550829 (11)	243386 (12)	25157135 (8)	50728497 (3)

1986 Classification

Palustrine Shrub	Palustrine Unconsolidated Bottom	Palustrine Unconsolidated Shore	Cultivated Rice	Lacustrine	Riverine	Agricultural	Urban	Upland Forested Plantation	Upland Rural Development	Other	Acreage Totals, 1986	
0 —	0 —	0 —	0 —	0 —	0 —	0 —	0 —	0 —	0 —	68 94	1770493 32	Marine Subtidal
0 —	0 —	0 —	0 —	0 —	0 —	0 —	0 —	0 —	24 98	930 50	133119 20	Marine Intertidal
0 —	107 68	0 —	0 —	1465 94	0 —	14 96	228 56	0 —	300 62	539 44	17637644 2	Estuarine Subtidal
0 —	0 —	0 —	0 —	0 —	0 —	0 —	0 —	0 —	0 —	0 —	29059 27	Estuarine Subtidal
436 85	482 48	35 94	0 —	495 94	43 95	7 96	1596 46	0 —	857 55	2544 32	3956914 4	Estuarine Emergents
0 —	118 56	0 —	0 —	0 —	0 —	442 70	864 51	0 —	909 57	116 89	666163 13	Estuarine Forested Shrub
0 —	33 62	0 —	0 —	9 94	0 —	0 —	245 58	0 —	231 93	2540 45	551377 11	Estuarine Unconsolidated Shore
7081 33	5578 37	58 98	444 99	87 90	203 75	1329 32	211 51	0 —	544 53	559 87	253718 12	Palustrine Aquatic Bed
940108 11	92038 13	3894 34	213024 26	141310 50	13152 63	516730 15	112439 67	20689 49	52373 3	34019 21	26383336 8	Palustrine Emergents
2825091 8	75365 21	693 75	38707 60	7792 49	30000 33	141723 21	65865 16	109821 27	82774 19	27817 19	51929552 3	Palustrine Forested
14328217 5	38051 15	337 61	19561 33	9285 43	14113 34	76256 20	37096 31	77773 32	30649 21	33090 52	17235180 4	Palustrine Shrub
14339 29	4333393 4	7152 82	5582 44	2495 35	4281 96	44581 32	12463 22	399 49	23438 33	73816 74	4615108 4	Palustrine Unconsolidated Bottom
5055 78	3616 23	348043 17	14 99	79 82	45 86	1813 37	7195 88	54 99	2075 54	2656 72	382188 16	Palustrine Unconsolidate Shore
38535 41	5212 31	0 —	11542972 10	1261 99	0 —	17811 33	8448 62	32690 46	13314 31	4244 57	11682848 10	Cultivated Rice
28373 75	5543 38	24547 78	28762 45	14383024 11	0 —	2489 98	7633 60	0 —	6193 42	2209 64	14608888 11	Lacustrine
119992 46	4147 87	123 85	206 77	0 —	6083767 9	2559 79	2217 100	0 —	1326 85	7196 65	6291128 10	Riverine
35921 46	371870 13	7964 35	703025 29	44978 40	39501 68							Agricultural
14 98	9001 16	596 53	0 —	2009 72	337 102							Urban
4440 37	23457 16	1488 80	79 98	7172 59	80 85							Upland Forested Plantation
1153 71	23868 39	3900 93	152 89	8481 46	2050 62							Upland Rural Development
16865 38	264851 13	15338 36	5405 35	115377 75	68344 51							Other
18365620 4	5256730 4	414168 15	12557932 10	14725320 11	6255916 9							Acreage Totals, 1997

Column group headers: Freshwater Habitats (Palustrine Shrub, Palustrine Unconsolidated Bottom, Palustrine Unconsolidated Shore); Cultivated Rice; Deepwater Habitats (Lacustrine, Riverine); Uplands (Agricultural, Urban, Upland Forested Plantation, Upland Rural Development, Other).

All photographs were taken by Tom Dahl, U.S. Fish and Wildlife Service, unless otherwise noted.